Stephen Gudeman

Note: Shading indicates fieldwork areas

Jamaica

Changing Jamaica

Changing Jamaica

Adam Kuper
Department of Anthropology
University College London

Routledge & Kegan Paul
London and Boston

First published in 1976
by Routledge & Kegan Paul Ltd
Broadway House, 68–74 Carter Lane
London EC4V 5EL and
9 Park Street
Boston, Mass. 02108, U.S.A.
Set in Monotype Plantin
and printed in Great Britain by
Redwood Burn Limited, Trowbridge & Esher

ISBN 0 7100 8241 X

For Goody

Contents

Contents

Illustrations

Tables

Map

Figure

Acknowledgments

I left Jamaica with numerous debts of hospitality and friendship. I could not have had a more liberal or helpful employer than the National Planning Agency, which gave me such freedom, to proceed as I saw fit, and to publish what I wanted. Dr Gladstone Bonnick and his staff were always ready to discuss problems and to help in any way, and they never made me feel that I was a merely temporary colleague. I also learnt a great deal from discussions with various experts, and I am grateful to those who allowed me to refer to unpublished material. I would particularly like to thank Dr Gladstone Bonnick, Mr Alvin Burnett, Mrs Gloria Cumper, the Rev. Lewis Davidson, C.B.E., Mrs Pearl Gammon, Professor Douglas Hall, Rabbi Bernard Hooker, Mr Marcel Knight, Mr John Levy, of the St Andrew's Settlement at Majesty Pen, Miss Megan McCloghlin, Dr Errol Miller, Professor Rex Nettleford, and Mr G. E. Tatham. The individual Jamaicans, throughout the country, who helped me and my family so generously, cannot all be listed here. It would also be unsuitable to use an occasion like this to recall the many personal friendships we formed, although they all contributed to the fun we had in Jamaica.

My greatest debt is to Professor M. G. Smith, who initiated my study and provided much wise guidance. His contribution to the understanding of Jamaican society, and his commitment to its reform, are well known, and he has recently been awarded the highest national honour. I would add only that my debt was greatly increased by the way in which he tolerated my occasional disagreements—indeed, he constantly encouraged me to develop my own ideas and to try out novel interpretations. He and Professor Edward Shils were also kind enough to read my report, and to suggest that I recast it for general publication.

London   ADAM KUPER

xi

Chapter 1

Introduction

In 1972 the Peoples' National Party won Jamaica's general election by a landslide, and came to office after a decade in opposition. The new government was determined to take radical political initiatives, and quickly began to commission studies of various sectors of the economy. Professor M. G. Smith, an adviser to the new government, suggested among other things that an anthropologist might usefully be commissioned to report on the tendencies of social change. I was given this unusual brief, and carried out fieldwork on the island for thirteen months from July 1972, while on attachment to the National Planning Agency in the Office of the Prime Minister. I presented my report to the government in March 1974, and this book is an adaptation of the report.

Jamaica is small enough, its social experience sufficiently coherent, to make the notion of an anthropological account just plausible; an anthropological account in the sense of a study which relies above all on one observer's personal experience of various social situations as the basis for an analysis of a total social system. The rationale for an anthropological approach is perhaps best phrased in terms of the value of immersion in a local culture, together with the advantages of a perspective which derives from a thorough training in cross-cultural studies. The objective, an openness to local values, combined with a critical perspective on them, is perhaps most easily achieved by a foreign social scientist. Jamaican studies have too often failed to achieve the necessary distancing from Jamaican folk-models and values, which are seldom properly understood as a system of action in their own right, which demands the same objective and systematic spirit as the economist or demographer brings to other social facts.

I carried out fieldwork at four 'sites'. To begin with, I made a

1

study of a rural village in north Manchester, in the hills in the centre of the island. Next came Kingston, where a quarter of Jamaica's population is crowded. Here I tried to combine field-work by day in the slums of West Kingston with fieldwork in the early evenings among my civil service colleagues, the middle-class and expatriate families near my suburban home, and the Jewish community. Then to Montego Bay, where I investigated the social implications of the tourist industry. Finally, I spent a month on Jamaica's largest sugar estate where, if anywhere, the old Jamaica is insistently brought to mind, but in a harsh and decaying guise.

These studies provided fresh raw material, but they cumulatively provided me with something at least equally important. From the experience of fieldwork I developed a feel for contemporary Jamaica, and derived some of the insights one needs for the critical use of secondary sources—richly available in this case, if of uneven quality and coverage. Fieldwork gave me the 'anthro-pological' perspective I had been groping after. Through a first-hand attempt to understand various particular, contemporary Jamaican social circumstances, I came to some sort of under-standing of the meaning and functions of Jamaican models of social life; and so came to appreciate the perspective which imbued even some of the most sophisticated Jamaican analyses of Jamaican society.

While Jamaica does yield to an anthropological approach, I would not wish to overstate the social and cultural uniformity of the island. One can readily identify several distinctive forms of community in Jamaica: most obviously, perhaps, Kingston and its suburbs; the market towns; the tourist belt; the plantations; and the rural villages. These vary along a number of dimensions —economic complexity, social differentiation, the degree to which traditional modes of social relationship endure, and cultural development and variety. Moreover, throughout the island there are marked social and cultural distinctions between the remaining members of the plantocracy, the 'middle-class', the urban workers and lumpenproletariat, and the peasant farmers and agricultural labourers. However, by looking at these segments of the population above all in relation to one another, rather than in terms of their internal peculiarities, a general idea of Jamaican society can be formulated.

Jamaica is not only a complex society; it is a complex society undergoing economic and political transformation. Politically independent since 1962, the colonial political system of the last generation has been replaced with an effective two-party democracy. From a plantation-dominated agrarian society, Jamaica has become an industralizing society, one-third urban, and has swung from the traditional mercantilist dependence on Britain to a more contemporary and sophisticated (if no less one-sided) involvement with North American capital and markets.

These developments are easy enough to chart. The problems they raise, however, are extremely complex. First of all, the changes in social relationships which have accompanied these political and economic transformations must in some way be conceptualized and analysed. This is perhaps my central problem in this book. One can turn for descriptions of a slightly earlier period to the work of Jamaican anthropologists, particularly M. G. Smith, Edith Clarke and Fernando Henriques.[1] I also have my own field-material, the rather meagre publications of the recent students of Jamaican society, and the various, mainly statistical, materials published by the government.

Social and economic historians have provided valuable studies of the slave society and of the immediate post-emancipation period,[2] but unfortunately they have left a serious gap in our understanding of the years of direct colonial rule, from 1865 to 1944. The neglect of this period both reflects and reinforces the obsession with the 'anti-society' of slave Jamaica, which still provides the point of reference for many contemporary students of Jamaica. This gap is therefore a handicap to the understanding of social change in modern Jamaica. There can be no doubt that the continuities with Jamaica under slavery have generally been exaggerated. The nineteenth century saw major changes, perhaps the most important being the emergence of a substantial and reasonably prosperous peasant sector and of a coloured, urban middle-class.[3] These developments have been studied in their earlier stages, but the period of direct colonial rule was not one of economic and social stability. Although the social changes in this period are inadequately documented, one can still confidently stress the rapid acceleration in the rate of change after the Second World War. Certainly many Jamaicans have found it difficult to adjust to the transformations witnessed in the past generation, and particularly in the past decade.

In writing this essay I was determined not to be content with a study of changes in the social structure, or of the effects upon social relations of political and economic developments since the war. However intimidating, such a project would obviously fail to cope with the realities. Economic processes and, even more, political developments are shaped by the social structure which they will in turn affect; and, of course, political and economic developments are themselves closely inter-related.

My aim is to sketch a total analysis of contemporary Jamaican society; to suggest the ways in which political, economic and social relationships, and actors' models, are articulated with each other in a changing and dynamic fashion. A hopeless task, and one for which I am not properly equipped. Yet a task that must be attempted; the alternative is to be merely academic, for the sign of the merely academic is its distance from the complexities of real life.

For those unfamiliar with Jamaica, a brief introductory account may be helpful. Columbus discovered the island in 1494 and, after a period of Spanish occupation, British forces took Jamaica in 1655. Sugar production began, and for a time in the eighteenth century Jamaica was the world's largest sugar producer. The small native Indian population was thrust aside, and disappeared; the Spaniards were expelled; and the British settlers brought in large numbers of African slaves to grow the sugar. By 1775 nearly half a million slaves had been brought to Jamaica, and although the mortality was terrible, there were in 1820 about 340,000 slaves as against 35,000 whites and perhaps the same number of 'free coloured' people, manumitted slaves, often of mixed black-white parentage. The 'free coloureds' were granted civil rights only shortly before the emancipation of the slaves in 1834. Experiments to replace slave labour with half-free 'apprentices' and Indian indentured labourers were unsuccessful, and in the second half of the nineteenth century the sugar estates continued the decline which had begun before the end of slavery. At the same time, a viable class of peasant farmers grew up, refugees from the plantations who colonized undeveloped areas of the island. The white oligarchy, economically vulnerable now, failed politically in its attempt to come to terms with the free blacks and the emerging coloured middle-class. After traumatic riots at Morant Bay in 1865, and their brutal suppression, Jamaica became a Crown Colony.

During the new colonial period, minor political reforms were introduced, bananas joined sugar as a major export crop, and the island gradually declined in strategic significance and economic weight. The depression of the 1930s brought about a sharp decline in prices, and in the demand for migrant labour. In 1938 there were serious labour disturbances throughout the British West Indies, and in Jamaica a new nationalist movement developed side by side with trade unions. In 1944 elections were held on the basis of universal suffrage, and a ministerial form of government established. In 1962 full independence was granted. In the post-war decades, too, the mining of bauxite began on a large scale, the tourist industry expanded, and a secondary industry sector developed. The large plantations were rationalized and passed into the hands of foreign concerns.

In 1970 the population of Jamaica was 1,865,000, the vast majority being of African origin. The island is the largest of the former British West Indian island territories, but with an area of only 4,411 square miles it is dwarfed by its neighbours, Cuba and Hispaniola. In 1969, according to figures published by the United Nations, Jamaica's rate of natural increase was the fifteenth highest in the world. At the same time, Jamaica was high in the economic growth league of developing countries. In the decade 1952–63 Jamaica achieved the world's highest per capita increase in productivity, but the distribution of wealth is radically unbalanced.

Part one

Population and Economy

Chapter 2

The Population of Jamaica

The modern transformation of Jamaican society is evident in the massive shift of its base, the distribution of the population. At an increasing pace over the past fifty years, the cities and the towns have grown at the expense of the countryside. As recently as 1943, only 18 per cent of Jamaica's population lived in Kingston and its suburbs (the 'Corporate Area'). In 1970 the Corporate Area contained 27 per cent of the total population. At the same time, thirteen other towns accounted for a further 10 per cent of the population; and if Kingston had been growing quickly, the pace in the other towns was even faster. Between 1960 and 1970 the overall average growth rate of Jamaica's population was 1·46 per cent per annum. The Corporate Area grew at a rate of 3 per cent per annum in this decade, Montego Bay and May Pen at a rate of 6 per cent per annum, and Spanish Town at the astonishing rate of 11 per cent per annum, almost overtaking Montego Bay in total population and thus becoming once again Jamaica's second city. Virtually all the rural parishes grew in population at a rate of less than 1 per cent per annum in the 1960s, but even in the rural areas the patches of mining and tourist development have shown much greater than average population increases.

In short, rural Jamaicans have been streaming into the towns and the places of opportunity. Natural increase in the cities is lower than in Jamaica as a whole, and virtually all the dramatic growth in the urban population is attributable to internal migration. It was estimated, on the basis of the 1960 census, that 44 per cent of Jamaicans over the age of 14 had lived in more than one parish.[1]

People have not only been converging on the cities. Migration abroad (at first particularly to Cuba and Panama) has a long history in Jamaica, but since 1943 emigration has completely

9

eclipsed immigration and re-immigration. Emigration to Britain had many of the features of a millenarian cult in the 1950s and 1960s, and in these decades 200,000 Jamaicans emigrated. In several recent years recorded migration from Jamaica exceeded 20,000, or more than 1 per cent of the total population. Since the virtual closure of entry to Britain, migrants have mainly been going to the USA and Canada. New legislation in these countries allowed the stream of migration to gather force once again, and in 1969 Jamaica's net loss from migration was officially recorded as being 29,000. This was the peak, but even in 1972 13,400 Jamaicans went to live in the USA, and 2,800 in Canada. These are the legal migrants—there are others. [2]

This high rate of emigration in recent decades has helped to mitigate the effects of what would otherwise have been the extremely grave consequences of the third major change in the demographic structure of Jamaica—the rapid growth in the rate of natural increase, due in part to a general rise in standards of living and care. Jamaica has only entered the modern phase of rapid population growth fairly recently. In the period between the censuses of 1921 and 1943, as many people were added to the total population as had been gained in the sixty years up to 1921. [3] Between 1969 and 1972 the rate of natural increase fluctuated between 26·8 and 27·5 per thousand per annum. It is possible that there is now a slight downward trend in the birth-rate, but this has been matched by an improvement in the death-rate, and particularly in the rate of infant mortality.

It is easy enough, in a crude fashion, to see the way in which migration has affected the growth of the population. Between 1969 and 1971, for example, net migration removed more than half as many people as were added to the population by natural increase. It is difficult to work out specific predictions, however, or even very detailed analyses, since migration statistics have consistently proved to be underestimates, and it is not clear whether or not children regularly join their parents or older siblings abroad. However, at least one unpleasant consequence is now emerging from the combination of a high birth-rate and a high rate of adult migration. In 1911, children under 14 years of age represented less than 40 per cent of the population. In 1960, the proportion was almost the same. But, in 1970, 45 per cent of Jamaica's population was under 14 years of age. This not only means that heavier demands must be made on the adult, working population. Unless a large proportion of these youngsters emigrate, there is very shortly going to be an enormous jump in the size of Jamaica's population.

There is no mystery about these movements of population. The rural population has been concentrated on smallholdings which can no longer support an increase in population without a substantial drop in the standard of living. At the same time, the cities have been booming. Unemployment in the cities is high, but as I shall show, the chances of at least intermittent but highly-paid employment are reasonably good. For the bulk of rural children, the choice is obvious. The movement abroad from Jamaica, although at first based on inadequate information (and given false encouragement by the comparatively healthy condition of the British economy in the 1950s), is no less obviously based on a reasonable economic assessment of the possibilities.

Unfortunately, the social effects of large-scale migration on children and others left behind have not been studied. Social workers in Kingston reported a high proportion of their case-load involving children whose parents live abroad, but it is possible that the dislocation has been less than might have been expected, given the huge numbers involved. There are no ghost towns in Jamaica, and the relationships between children and foster-parents in Jamaica, and parents abroad, are often adequate. Studies in other parts of the world suggest that labour migration need not disrupt the life of the community which remains behind, and a recent study in the Caribbean, of the extreme situation in Montserrat, stressed the continuities and successful adaptations.[4]

Nevertheless some of the consequences of the migrations abroad can be studied in detail, and I shall discuss them here more fully since they bring to light a number of the central issues which face contemporary Jamaica. In an analysis of the economic effects of the migration to Britain, one scholar concluded that on the whole Jamaica's economic development had benefited. First of all population pressure was reduced—'Total population was probably 200,000 less in 1962 than it would have been without emigration.' Second, although a disproportionate number of skilled workers emigrated, so depressing total production, per capita production probably increased, as did the rate of employment. And third, he suggested that the remittances of the migrants were an important source of foreign exchange.[5] (This continues to be true. The Bank of Jamaica estimated that in 1972 remittances from Jamaicans abroad totalled J$40 million.)

It is no longer possible to be so sanguine. The change in direction of migration—from Britain to North America—has been accompanied by a change in the type of migrant. The migration to the United Kingdom was massive, rapid, and un-selective. In the seven years to 1962 alone (the year in which restrictions were first imposed), over 150,000 Jamaicans went to live in Britain. Although various surveys suggest that the emigrants were on the whole more skilled, more experienced in urban employment, and perhaps better educated than the average Jamaican, none the less this migration certainly included large numbers of unskilled and unemployed men and women.[6] The picture of the North American migration is very different.

The new USA immigration laws, enacted in 1965, which came into force in 1968, placed Jamaica in a Western hemisphere group of countries which was permitted a total of 120,000 immigrants a year. Jamaica has taken an extraordinarily high proportion of these places—well over 10 per cent in several years. Under the new regulations, immigrants fall into two main categories. Some are allowed into the USA because they have a parent, child or spouse there. The others are admitted if they are awarded 'labour certificates', and special categories of workers are favoured. Most Jamaicans are admitted because of family connections—the earlier, less dramatic but long-term exodus to the USA is paying off now. In 1971, of 12,000 or so granted entry to the USA, only 1,885 had labour certificates, most of them women, mainly domestic servants but also nurses.

Two consequences of these arrangements are beneficial to Jamaica. First of all, more women than men are migrating, so slightly dampening the future rise in the birth-rate.[7] Second, nearly 43 per cent of the migrants were aged under twenty in 1972, and in general a large number of young people are leaving (after, it is true, having had their education subsidized by Jamaica).

A third consequence is, however, more worrying. The level of skill in the migrating population is very much higher than in the Jamaican population as a whole. It may be that the immigration procedures are deliberately biased in order to skim off the skilled people, but it is possible that this is at least in part an unintended consequence of the legislation. Perhaps Jamaicans with families in the USA were assisted by them to rise occupationally and educationally; perhaps the earlier migrants to the USA were in any case from higher-status families. In any case, the facts are clear. In 1972, of 13,427 migrants to the USA, 6,311 were workers and 7,116 were dependents. Less than a third of the workers had qualified for labour certificates, but nevertheless only 30 per cent of the workers who emigrated were unskilled or only semi-skilled. Sixteen per cent fell into the top bracket of professional, technical, administrative and managerial personnel; 14 per cent were clerical or sales workers; and 40 per cent were craftsmen and skilled workers.

In the case of the Canadian emigration, the bias in favour of skilled personnel is deliberate government policy. Moreover, fewer dependents are admitted. While more than half of the Jamaicans who go to the USA are dependents, this is true of only about 40 per cent of those who go to Canada. Table 1 compares the proportion of workers in various categories in Jamaica, with those in the groups of emigrants to North America.

TABLE 1 *Workers in Jamaica and emigrating to North America: percentage distributions* [8]

| | | Emigrating to | |
	Jamaica (1967)	USA (1972)	Canada (1971)
Professional, technical and managerial	6	16	11
Clerical and sales	11	14	24
Craftsmen and skilled workers	18	40	36
Semi-skilled and unskilled workers	65	30	28
Total	100	100	99

It is evident that whether or not the USA is following Canada's deliberate policy and concentrating upon the recruitment of economically desirable immigrants, emigration from Jamaica is biased in favour of the very people whose services Jamaica needs most. The less-skilled workers, whom Jamaica has in overabundance, cannot take advantage of the opportunities to seek their fortunes elsewhere. The less-skilled and unskilled workers who represent two-thirds of Jamaica's work-force, contribute under a third to the migrant total.

In fact the situation is even more serious than these gross statistics suggest, for among the most highly-trained the drain is already critical. A recent study showed that in 1967, Jamaica produced 610 university graduates. In the same year 780 graduates emigrated, and only about 100 returned to the island. In the following year, too, there was a net loss of university graduates.[9] The same study estimated the investment gain to the receiving countries from the immigration of 710 Jamaican university graduates in 1968 at about US $10 million.[10] Of course, Jamaica is partly compensated by the immigration of foreign graduates, but this is both incomplete and unsatisfactory. They are less likely to devote a lifetime's work to Jamaica, and cannot provide the leadership Jamaica might expect from her own university-trained citizens. At slightly lower levels, however, Jamaica cannot afford to compete with developed countries for skilled non-professionals to replace those she is losing.

According to the projections of manpower balances for 1975 made in the second five-year plan, two categories of workers will be in short supply. There will be a deficit (as a percentage of supply) of over 22 per cent in the professional, managerial and technical category; and a deficit of over 36 per cent in the category of craftsmen and skilled workers. All other categories will be in oversupply—semi-skilled and unskilled workers by 45 per cent.

Thus while the earlier stages of the post-war migratory movement abroad may have been to Jamaica's benefit, at least from the economic point of view, the more recent phase has been increasingly disadvantageous. It is one of the paradoxes of under-development that the poorer countries subsidize the training of professionals for the rich countries.

To sum up, the demographic framework of Jamaican society exhibits most of the features familiar in underdeveloped societies throughout the world, but perhaps in a more extreme form than many—the strong tidal movement from the farms to the towns and to Kingston, so that an agrarian and rural society has become well over one-third urban within a generation; the high rate of population growth, limited only by emigration; and, finally, the development of a 'brain drain' so severe that Jamaica is probably exporting each year more graduates than it produces, and as many skilled workers as it will need in the year to come. All these movements both reflect and generate enormous social changes. They are a function, also, of economic development; but each of these movements is potentially fatal to the further economic development of Jamaica.

Chapter 3

The Economy

Jamaica is one of the few new states to enjoy rapid economic growth. The transition to political self-government came at a time when British investment in the country was yielding pride of place to the United States and Canada, and investment from these countries was made above all in the new growth industries, bauxite and tourism. Bauxite mining in particular has become a mainstay of the Jamaican economy. During the 1960s Jamaica emerged as the world's largest supplier of bauxite (the raw material for aluminium), and produced over 20 per cent of the world's consumption. The tourist industry has also expanded remarkably, and stimulated by the bauxite and tourist developments, the construction industry has enjoyed high levels of activity. The government has encouraged the development of secondary industries, and here too its success has been greater than expected. But there are three serious drawbacks in this success story. First of all, the agricultural sector has been extremely disappointing, barely marking time during the recent period of rapid industrial development and population growth. Second, employment opportunities have failed to keep pace with population growth. And third, as a consequence of high unemployment and the retardation of the agricultural sector, the very unequal distribution of wealth has not improved: it may even have got worse. The economists debate whether or not this is all a matter of growing pains, or whether in fact economic development in Jamaica has serious structural deficiencies.

The dominance of the new mining sector over the traditional export standby, sugar, is overwhelming. In 1972, bauxite and alumina earned more than three times as much as agricultural exports.[1] It is perhaps even more surprising to see the extent to which manufacturing has overtaken agriculture. In 1959, manufacturing industry for the first time overtook the contribution made by the agricultural sector to the Gross Domestic Product. In 1972, agriculture, forestry and fishing contributed only 9 per cent of GDP, while manufacturing contributed 14 per cent. As recently as 1950, agriculture was contributing over 30 per cent to Jamaica's GDP.

TABLE 2 *Jamaica's Gross Domestic Product and its components, 1968 and 1972*[2]

	1968		1972	
	J$ million	%	J$ million	%
Agriculture, forestry and fishing	77·5	10	105·6	9
Mining, quarrying and refining	100·1	13	141·1	12
Manufacturing	115·3	15	165·5	14
Construction and installation	94·9	12	130·9	11
Distributive trades	102·3	13	160·3	14
Financial institutions	35·0	4	76·8	7
Public administration	69·7	9	108·6	10
Other	189·8	24	268·8	23
Total	784·6	100	1,157·6	100

It is estimated that Jamaica's GDP grew at an annual rate of 10 per cent between 1950 and 1968 at factor cost. If the effect of rising prices is eliminated, the annual growth rate in this period was 6·7 per cent.[3] However, the differential rate of growth between various sectors of the economy was great. In 1950, agriculture contributed 32 per cent to total GDP; in 1972, only 9 per cent. At the same time, mining, virtually nonexistent in 1950, contributed 12 per cent in 1972, and both construction and manufacturing increased their percentage contribution to GDP. Throughout this period, however, rural Jamaicans have remained in the majority. Nearly two-thirds of the Jamaican population still lives in the rural areas, for the rapid growth of the modern industrial sector has not been matched by an equivalent growth in urban employment. In 1972, manufacturing industry employed only 12·7 per cent of the work-force, and although this was an improvement over previous years, employment in this sector was not even keeping pace with the growth of the work-force. Bauxite mining, so powerful a factor in the economy, employs only a few thousand workers, and the tourist industry itself only claims directly to employ 12,000 workers.[4]

TABLE 3   *Industrial distribution of classifiable labour force, percentages*[5]

Sector	1960	1968
Agriculture, forestry, fishing	38·7	33·8
Mining, etc.	0·7	1·3
Construction and installation	7·2	7·3
Manufacturing	9·1	11·1
Public utilities	0·5	0·8
Commerce (distribution)	9·9	11·7
Transport, communication, storage	2·8	3·4
Miscellaneous services	21·8	21·4
Public administration	7·6	9·2
Unspecified	1·7	—
Total	100	100

In short, the new centres of Jamaica's wealth do not employ many Jamaicans; and the old, declining agricultural sector still dominates the employment picture. It has been estimated that in 1958, average urban income in Jamaica was 2·4 times larger than in rural areas. The current estimate is that average urban income is now four times greater.[6]

These internal structural imbalances in Jamaica's economy are related to its dependence on foreign investment. Jamaican politicians have been able to give some nudges to the economy, but the direction of economic development has been shaped by the investment decisions of large foreign companies. According to one authority, foreign ownership:[7]

ranges from 100 per cent in bauxite-alumina, to 40 per cent in sugar and its by-products, 40 per cent of transport, communications and public utilities combined, about 60 per cent of financial services and 55 per cent of hotel capacity in the tourist industry.

The scale of most of the crucial enterprises demands either great foreign concerns, or direct government intervention. To date, only the now unprofitable sugar lands have been turned over to the government—eagerly sold off to them by British sugar interests. The bauxite industry has recently been directly challenged on the meagre royalty payments it has been making, and a new, substantial levy has been imposed. Overall, however, Jamaica has been too dependent on foreign investment to interfere with the present neo-colonial pattern.

Another way of looking at Jamaica's problem is to consider its balance of payments. During the modern period of rapid economic growth, the balance of trade has been consistently unfavourable. In 1972, for example, imports were J$493·2 million, while exports were J$300·3 million, leaving a deficit on visible trade of J$192·9 million. Food imports alone rose in value from J$45·9 million in 1969, to J$71·3 million in 1972. The shortfall on the balance of payments is partly met through receipts from tourism, capital inflow, and receipts from Jamaicans abroad. However, these inflows are partly counterbalanced by invisible imports, mainly freight and insurance, and the payment of dividends and repayment of loans. The crucial factor in the equation then becomes 'investor confidence', for during periods of uncertainty there are huge capital outflows. In the past the varying capital requirements of the bauxite industry were of greater importance, but the present situation is that other sources of foreign investment are vital. In 1972, the deficit on current account was partly balanced by a net inflow of J$117·1 million, including a net inflow of J$94·8 million in private funds—but this was much less than in previous years. Jamaica is in deficit in its trade with all three of its major trading partners, the USA (which now dominates Jamaica's foreign trade), the United Kingdom and Canada. However, Jamaica is greatly increasing its exports—particularly of manufactured goods—to the Caribbean Free Trade Area, and in relation to this market it occupies a much more favourable position, politically and economically. In 1974 Jamaica courageously imposed a levy of over J $200 million on the bauxite companies, and this will alleviate some of the problems, while unfortunately not affecting the underlying structural and political imbalances.

The fundamental problem is, in short, that while the economy as a whole has recently been growing at a good rate, development has been concentrated in a few sectors, including some—mining and tourism—which make little impact on the earnings of all but a very few Jamaicans. Moreover, development in these sectors does little to encourage development in others, aside from a probably short-term effect on the construction industry. The bulk of Jamaica's population is still settled in the rural areas, and it is here that development has been least significant.

Chapter 4

Agriculture

The position of agriculture in the Jamaican economy has shifted drastically in the post-war years. As recently as 1938, the agricultural sector accounted for 36 per cent of Jamaica's Gross Domestic Product; in 1972, for only 9 per cent. At the same time, however, its share of the 'classifiable labour force' declined from 45 per cent in 1943, to 34 per cent in 1972, not nearly enough to compensate for the decline in relative productivity. Moreover, in the 1970s nearly two-thirds of Jamaica's population still lived in the rural areas, most of them on agricultural smallholdings.

The impoverishment of the agricultural sector has not been matched by major alterations in its structure; indeed, while the articulation of agriculture in the economic structure of Jamaica has been revolutionized, the internal structure of the sector has been remarkably stable. After the abolition of slavery, there developed a dual agricultural economy, for side by side with the large estates there grew up a considerable sector of small-scale peasant holdings. One can trace these back into the slave era itself, when slaves were encouraged to feed themselves from their own, specially allocated gardens, and allowed to trade any surplus, but the difference in scale and independence of peasant farming in the latter part of the nineteenth century was very significant.[1] The large estates, then as now, concentrated on export crops and depended heavily on seasonal labour. The small peasant farmers mainly produced food-crops for consumption and sale, but were also dependent often on other sources of income—notably seasonal labour on the plantations.

In 1968, there were only 994 farms of over 100 acres—0·54 per cent of all farms. However, farms in this category covered nearly 55 per cent of all farm acreage. For their part, most

21

peasant farmers have very small farms. In 1968 the national average farm size was just over 8 acres. Small farms under 25 acres accounted for 98 per cent of all farms, but covered only 37 per cent of farm acreage. [2]

Until the last war, these large estates were generally in the hands of either local planters or absentee landlords, who allowed their estates to be managed by local men. After the war, there was increasing concentration of such large estates in the hands of vast industrial concerns, notably Tate and Lyle, the bauxite companies, and the government itself.

The farms of medium size (between 25 and 200 acres) occupy only about 12 per cent of total farm acreage, and are as yet of little particular economic significance. A high proportion of them appear to be badly-run, and looked upon as simply part-time occupations for members of the Jamaican middle-class, who work in the towns or own businesses locally. Farming cane and bananas on the coast, and livestock, potatoes, pimento and coffee in the interior, the owners of such farms have to a considerable extent taken over the leadership of rural Jamaica from the old 'plantocrats'. Together with the managers of commercial estates and the local professionals they are now the dominant figures in rural society.

At the other end of the scale, there has been an absolute decline in the viability of peasant holdings. The number of farms of over 5 acres has dropped, while the number of farms of under 5 acres has increased. At the same time, the acreage of farmland overall declined. There are various reasons for this, but the main cause has been the alienation of farmland to bauxite companies and (to a far lesser extent) to land speculators. The acquisition of land by bauxite companies and government has resulted in a further decline in the demand for rural labour (begun with the gradual mechanization of the sugar estates), since the lands acquired were often neglected, or put into capital-intensive forms of production such as ranching. [3] Thus the traditional sources of extra income for the peasant, agricultural labour and the leasing of land (often, however, in rather disadvantageous share-cropping deals) have been reduced.

Successive government plans have attempted to halt the impoverishment of the small farmer. Until recently, none showed success. In fact the reduction in land held by small farmers has occurred while successive governments have carried through a variety of land redistribution schemes. Between 1929 and 1971, a total of 173,835 acres was allocated in 39,381 parcels—i.e. the equivalent of nearly 12 per cent of the total acreage in farms in 1968.[4] Recently, however, a new scheme has been introduced, which shows signs of success. Government is leasing estates, and its own lands, to small farmers to supplement their holdings to a reasonable level; and this sensible and modest programme has been enthusiastically supported, despite the warnings of the self-styled experts on the psychology of the 'small man' in Jamaica, who confidently asserted that he was not interested in leasehold. Modelled on a scheme successfully introduced by Alcan, the bauxite company, on its own lands, 'Operation Land-lease' is perhaps the most hopeful development in Jamaican agriculture for a generation.

As in many developing countries, so in Jamaica productivity per acre tends to vary *inversely* with farm size. Although the larger farmers have the advantages of economies of scale, mechanization and sophisticated management (at least potentially), and although in general they hold the best land, they are consistently out-produced by the small farmer. The small farmer has all the necessary labour to hand, and also has the incentive to exploit his land to the full. Indeed, he generally over-exploits it, with consequent deterioration. While the large farmers constantly complain of a shortage of labour (a phenomenon I shall discuss later), the small farmer, whose labour is cheap because it has no alternative productive outlet, is at a considerable advantage. Another reason is that the small farmer concentrates on food-crops, which are more labour-intensive and in general more profitable per acre than export crops.[5]

Although the small farms occupy the lesser share of Jamaica's farmlands, they employ the larger part of agriculture labour. The 1960 population census showed that approximately 51 per cent of workers employed in agriculture were employers or own-account workers, 41 per cent were employees, and 7 per cent were unpaid family workers. Since nearly 98 per cent of all farms are under 25 acres, we can safely assume that virtually all the employers, self-employed and unpaid family workers must have been working on these small farms. On the other hand, most employees must have been on larger farms and estates. Thus it is safe to conclude

23

that farms of under 25 acres employed about 58 per cent of those working in agriculture in Jamaica in 1960.

The relative productivity of the large and small farms is more difficult to gauge, since the large farms concentrate on export crops, while the small farms are generally planted with food crops. Farms over 100 acres in size derive only between 3 and 9 per cent of their income from food-crops, while food-crops contribute a third to a half of the agriculture income of the small farmers (plus subsistence). However, it is not too much to say that the small farms feed Jamaica.

A few statistics may underline this point. In 1968, farms of under 25 acres occupied 38 per cent of the farm acreage in Jamaica, and 56 per cent of the cultivated acreage. Thus they were more intensively farmed. They were also farmed to a greater degree in mixed stand, and they included a wide range of crops. Unfortunately (though understandably) the agricultural statistics deal mainly with crops farmed in pure stand, and so tend to underestimate the contribution of these small farms. However, even of crops farmed in pure stand, the small farms provided 96 per cent of Jamaica's yams, 84 per cent of her Irish potatoes, 91 per cent of her pigs, 94 per cent of her goats, and 84 per cent of her poultry. These are most of the staple foods of the country. The only comparable contribution of the large estates was in their production of beef, in any case a luxury food. At the same time, farms of under 25 acres made a considerable contribution to export agriculture (or at least, to the production of export-type crops for the Jamaican market). In 1968, the small farmers produced 17 per cent of the sugar cane farmed in pure stand, 31 per cent of the citrus, 68 per cent of bananas, 85 per cent of cocoa, and 86 per cent of the coffee.

There can be little doubt that farms of under 25 acres (with only 38 per cent of Jamaica's farm acreage) made a greater contribution to the Gross Domestic Product than did the larger farms and estates. In 1972, export agriculture contributed 2·4 per cent of GDP, livestock and hunting 1·8 per cent, and domestic agriculture 3·8 per cent. Nor is it necessarily true that the large estates must be maintained because of their contribution to the balance of trade. Export agriculture was worth J$62·5 million in 1972, while food imports cost Jamaica J$71·3 million (or, less imports of meat, fish and meat and fish products, J$42·9 million).

It is therefore a matter of wonder that attempts to develop the small-farming sector are phrased mainly, still, in social terms—particularly in terms of the bogey of migration to the cities. There would seem to be a strong economic argument for extending the land held in this sector, at the expense of the old estate sector. However, at this stage there is much that can be done without radical restructuring. According to the Land Development and Utilization Commission there was in 1972 an extraordinary amount of idle, arable land in large farms. Farms of 100 acres and over had more than 100,000 arable acres, or nearly 12 per cent of their total acreages, lying idle. This would accommodate 10,000 viable small farms, or would increase the acreage of *cultivable land* available to small farmers by over 30 per cent. 'Operation Land-lease' is a start in the right direction.

Chapter 5

Employment and Migration to the Towns

Jamaica's modern economic growth has taken place in parts of the cities, the tourist belt, and the mining areas. Rural Jamaica has become relatively much poorer while these areas have been booming. At the same time, there has been a massive shift of population from the rural areas, into these locations of development and also abroad. But although the new sectors of the economy continue to be profitable and to grow, they cannot offer new jobs at anything like the required rate. It was inevitable that such rapid, structural changes in the economy would create great problems of readjustment, but it seems that there is more to it than that. The nature of the structural changes has created, it is argued, 'structural unemployment' stabilized at a high level. There is no possible employment substitute for the peasant farming sector, which, however, the nature of economic development has rendered progressively less able to maintain its standard of return on labour and investment.

As in many developing countries, so in Jamaica, increased investment brings greater returns, and also higher wages—but does not have a major effect on employment. The bauxite industry is quite astonishingly capital-intensive, but even in manufacturing industry the effect of new investment on employment is disappointing. Manufacturing output in Jamaica grew at an average rate of 8·4 per cent per annum between 1950 and 1965—but at the same time employment in manufacturing grew at an average annual rate of only 4·1 per cent.[1] Wages did rise as productivity increased, however, though at a slower pace.[2]

It has been shown that in Jamaica immigration from rural areas to the towns increases in response to rises in urban wages, even if job opportunities are static.[3] There would not be much point in artificially restraining the rises in urban wages, since

26

while this might suppress rural–urban movement to some extent it would not result in the creation of significant numbers of new jobs. Indeed, it might even depress the numbers of new jobs, since the employed would have less money to spend on goods and services. After all (and this is a point too often neglected in Jamaica), the problem is unemployment, not simply unemployment in the towns.

The 'unemployment problem' is, of course, the staple of gloomy foreign commentators, and it is also perhaps the main bogey of middle-class Jamaica. It is widely believed that the high rate of unemployment, exacerbated by a wasteful and foolish migration of young people from the city, has created an urban crisis which is perhaps the greatest present danger to the security of the state. Indeed, people vie with each other to heighten the gloom. Educated Jamaicans today glibly assert that 'over 20 per cent of the population is unemployed', and add with sombre relish that this is an understatement, since most of the so-called employed are really underemployed. Add in 'disguised unemployment', they suggest, and a truly staggering picture will be revealed.

I would not wish to understate the human problem, but in fact a much less dreadful reading of the unemployment statistics is appropriate. The logic of this will emerge as the unemployment figures are broken down into their components, and analysed. At a later stage I shall return to the significance of the prophecies of doom, and to the underlying assumptions of the prophets (some of which will emerge later in this chapter).

The first point to grasp in demythologizing the employment figures is that Jamaica has one of the world's highest rates of female participation in the labour force; but, at the same time, partly because of the fashion in which the questions about labour force membership are phrased and interpreted, women contribute disproportionately to the total unemployment statistics. The labour force is officially defined as including anyone over 14 years of age who says in the week of the survey that he or she is employed or is looking for work. In October 1972, over 22 per cent of the labour force said they were unemployed and would like work (though they were not necessarily actively seeking jobs). However, 35 per cent of the female labour force was unemployed on this definition, as opposed to only 14 per cent of the male

27

TABLE 4   *Employment in Jamaica, October 1972. Employment and unemployment by age group and sex*

Sex	Age group	Employed	Labour force Unemployed Number	%	Total	% of workforce Total	Unemployed
Male	14–24	81,709	35,339	30	117,048	26	57
	25–34	78,208	11,185	13	89,393	19	18
	35–54	140,837	10,238	7	151,075	33	16
	55 and over	93,949	5,259	5	99,208	22	9
	Sub-total	394,703	62,021	14	456,724	100	100
Female	14–24	42,400	50,521	54	92,921	26	43
	25–34	52,087	30,250	37	82,337	24	25
	35–54	94,618	30,365	24	124,983	36	25
	55 and over	42,705	8,620	17	51,325	14	7
	Sub-total	231,810	119,756	34	351,566	100	100
	Total	626,513	181,777	22·5	808,290		

(Source: *Economic Survey, 1972*)

labour force. But a very high proportion of women *were* in employment, by international standards: 38 per cent of all women in Jamaica over the age of 14.

If unemployment among men was 14 per cent, on this very liberal definition, its incidence was further concentrated in an interesting fashion within the male labour force. The young were worst off—57 per cent of the unemployed men were aged 14–24, although they accounted for only 26 per cent of the total male labour force. Among men over 35, by contrast, the unemployment rate in October 1972 was only 6 per cent. They represented 55 per cent of the total male labour force, but only 25 per cent of unemployed men. Another way of exposing the situation is to consider the problems of the 'inexperienced unemployed'—those who had never held a job, a category which does not overlap completely with the young. In 1968, according to the Labour Force Survey, the 'inexperienced unemployed' accounted for only 6 per cent of the total labour force in Kingston (both sexes), but for over 24 per cent of the unemployed there. Thus there appears to be a segment of the work force, partly but not entirely made up of very young men, who constituted the overwhelming majority of unemployed men. They can be identified with even greater precision: they tend to be urban-born.

In 1960, the population of Kingston and St Andrew was made up of 57 per cent native born and 43 per cent born elsewhere in Jamaica or abroad. However, the native born accounted for 65 per cent of the men in town looking for a first job.[4] In the island as a whole, in 1960, people who had moved into a town contributed 56 per cent of those in manufacturing industry; 54 per cent of those in construction; 62 per cent of those in electricity, water, transport and communication; 62 per cent of those in personal service; 68 per cent of those in commerce; and 77 per cent of those in other services.[5] Thus contrary to current myths, those moving into town had much better employment records than the urban born.

It may be that employers prefer more tractable workers from country areas, but it also seems to be true that the urban-born Jamaicans will only take relatively pleasant and lucrative jobs, because they have alternative forms of income through 'scuffling' (various more or less shady activities), occasional fishing, relatives, etc. People in such circumstances freely spurn a job offering, say,

J$12 a week as 'slavery'; but when the labour force survey comes round they can truthfully say that they would like a job—on the proper terms.

Various statistics help to pinpoint the location of unemployment even more precisely. Surveys of poor urban areas in Kingston show that household income is not related to household size.[6] This suggests that households are set up by and large by wage-earners, and that almost every wage-earner has his or her own household. The 1960 census figures tend to confirm this surmise, since they revealed that very few household heads were in the position of looking for their first jobs—only 5 per cent of the men and 6 per cent of the women in this category.[7] It seems likely, therefore, that the total male unemployment figures are swelled by a tendency of urban-born men to delay entry into wage-employment until they have to support a woman and children. An alternative view might be that they delay forming serious attachments until they are old enough to get the better urban jobs. Whichever explanation is correct, a recognition of the real incidence of serious unemployment within the work force greatly reduces the horror of the gross figures.

Perhaps this sounds smug and unfeeling: I do not mean it to be. On the contrary, a fuller understanding of the meaning of the unemployment figures must direct attention to the real centres of urban misery. It is not the young men who suffer most, though they frighten the middle-classes; it is the women.

In Jamaica a high proportion of households are headed by women, and this is particularly true in the poor urban areas. A survey in Trench Town, in Kingston, revealed 45 per cent of the households under women heads, only 19 per cent of whom had spouses living with them. In Delacree Pen, also in Kingston, women headed 39 per cent of the households, and only 17 per cent had spouses living with them (common-law or married partners).[8] Male-headed households are more likely to have four or more members, but it is clear that a large proportion of women and children in Kingston are dependent upon the wages of women. A few receive some money from fathers of illegitimate children, but this is an undependable, and generally small, source of extra income.

But one cannot begin to understand the significance of employment and unemployment in Kingston without taking the rest of the country into account at the same time. The basic fact of the situation was underlined by Francis, in his analysis of the 1960 census figures:[9]

> for both males and females the parishes of Kingston and St. Andrew have significantly lower percentages of their respective wage earners earning under £50 per annum, as compared with the corresponding percentages for Jamaica as a whole and all the other parishes. Whereas about 8·5 per cent of male wage earners and 19 per cent of female wage earners in the two parishes named earn less than fifty pounds per annum, the corresponding figures for most of the other parishes are about 30 and 55 per cent respectively.

Whatever the level of unemployment in Kingston, wage-earners in Kingston are well-off by the standards of the island as a whole, and certainly by comparison with the rural population. Moreover, although unemployment is a problem, rural migrants do better in finding employment than do the urban born. There is obviously a big 'pull' towards the towns in purely economic terms. There are various factors which at the same time 'push' the young rural-born Jamaican towards the town.

A striking feature of rural employment in Jamaica is that it is biased in favour of older people. A government publication recently remarked that 'surveys carried out in different areas indicate that the average age of farmers is usually over 50 years in a population in which 62 per cent are under 24 years of age'.[10] Early experience of land-leasing projects suggested that successful applicants would be in the older age-group; thus the average age of Alcan's tenants was 54.[11] On the plantations, too, the workers are overwhelmingly older men.

The myth which is widely invoked to explain such figures is the myth of foolish, headstrong youth, scorning the degrading and unprofitable tasks of their fathers in favour of the chimera of urban success. In fact two very concrete social processes explain the phenomenon rather better; one relates to farm-ownership, the other to agricultural wage-labour.

Virtually all Jamaican farmers are owner-occupiers, although in some cases the farmer is legally part-owner and custodian of

31

inalienable 'family land'.[12] The small farmer in Jamaica (as in many other countries—notably, perhaps, Ireland) is extremely reluctant to give shares in the land to his adult sons before his death or incapacity. Consequently, legal owners of farms are mainly older men. One result is that adult sons, with little to occupy them on their father's smallholding, will be tempted to seek their fortunes elsewhere. Another consequence is that whenever loans or leases are offered, as is customary, on the security of land-titles, these will go to older men. When, recently, the Jamaican government broke with the convention and allowed farming experience as a criterion for the allocation of leases, the average age of tenants declined from over 50 to under 40, clearly indicating that rural youth will take opportunities which are offered for own-account farming. These opportunities are rare, however, and the smallholder has little need for help on the average 8–9 acre farm. (Unpaid family workers account for only a little over 7 per cent of the rural labour force.) Even if the owner dies, the average farm cannot economically be divided, certainly not into more than two shares. Most children have no option but to leave the land.

But why do they not take the opportunities going a-begging (or so it is often said) on the plantations and large farms? There are two good reasons. First, such labour is paid a derisory wage, because the large estates are usually badly managed, and often unprofitable. Second, labour demand is highly seasonal. Of the 21,000 workers in sugar estates in 1972, 7,400 were employed only in the crop period, which lasts for half the year. Cane farmers employed a further 15,200 workers, and probably an even higher proportion of these were employed only during the crop. Moreover, the sugar estates guarantee only 100 days' work a year to registered workers, and this maximum appears to be close to the average. Most export crops have a similar, seasonal employment pattern. They are therefore attractive options only for small-holders, for whom the seasonal crop work coincides with the slack period for food-crops. They are not reasonable options for the man without a smallholding, who is free to compete for the much better-paid occasional work available in, for example, the construction industry, which would pay him more in one month than he would earn in a year of effective employment on a sugar estate.

This partly explains the high mean age of the estate workers—they are often smallholders, and therefore in any case older men, or they made their job choices before the new, industrial jobs became available after the war. There is another reason as well. On the sugar estates, the workers must be 'registered' by the companies before being granted such work as exists. Young workers are considered to be more troublesome, and therefore they are discriminated against. At the same time, the large estates have been mechanizing, and therefore registering fewer workers. More young men work in the factories, where jobs are less seasonal, marginally better-paid, and offer some prospects of training and advancement. The reasons so often cited for the drift from the estates—the stigma of sugar-labour, with its association with slavery, and the back-breaking nature of the work—are significant, but not sufficient to explain what is happening. After all, tens of thousands of young Jamaicans volunteer to cut cane in Florida every year, and in Jamaica a few progressive employers in the banana industry have demonstrated that reasonable conditions yield adequate and efficient labour.

In conclusion, something remains to be said about the intensity of employment in Jamaica, where much employment is casual or seasonal. In 1968 only 55 per cent of the male labour force had worked 40 hours or more in the week of the labour force survey. Twenty-four per cent had worked for less than 32 hours, 11 per cent for less than 16 hours. Moreover, of the total labour force, men and women, 41 per cent had worked for less than 10 months in the previous year, and 14 per cent for less than 6 months.

Underemployment is most common in the rural areas. According to the 1960 census, Kingston and St Andrew had the highest rate of unemployment in the country, but also the lowest percentage of persons underemployed. Thirteen per cent of workers in the Corporate Area were employed for 4 days or less in the survey week as against 24 per cent nationally and over 30 per cent in six rural parishes.[13] Seasonal lay-offs are also most significant in agriculture, though they do occur on a large scale in the construction and tourist industries. Thus the incidence of irregular employment tends to cancel out the higher rate of overall unemployment in the cities as against the country areas, adding further to the rationality of the landless young man's decision to go to Kingston.

Chapter 6

Economic Development and Social Change

Jamaica has been growing rapidly, and like an adolescent it seems ungainly and unco-ordinated. The outstanding structural weakness in her economic development can be summed up in the absence of those linkages which would feed development in one sector back into others. There are many reasons for this, perhaps most obviously the great extent of foreign control of investment, and the peculiar nature of the bauxite and tourist industries. The consequences have been serious, particularly for agricultural development. Migration to the cities, fed by the development of the new industries, has resulted in the creation of serious urban problems and the concentration of unemployment; but it has not greatly relieved the economic and social problems of the rural areas. Migration abroad, so long Jamaica's safety valve, has become a drain, since a growing proportion of the highly-skilled are leaving the island.

Economic developments and population movements on such a scale and in such a brief period are probably unparallelled in the history of Jamaica since the emancipation of the slaves. At that time new social classes emerged, with new interests, and the political organization of the society proved unable to cope with their demands. The balance of this book is concerned with the consequences of the modern transformation of Jamaica. Even with the material reviewed so far, however, one can begin to ask whether the nature and course of Jamaica's economic development has shaped a new set of class interests in the country. Who has benefited?

Between 1950 and 1968, Jamaica's real income per head grew at a rate of about 4·3 per cent per annum.[1] However, this new income was very unequally shared. A study based on 1958 figures estimated that in Jamaica the bottom 60 per cent of households

34

took only 19 per cent of the national income. The top 5 per cent of households took 30·2 per cent (see Table 5). The share of the

TABLE 5   *Income distribution in Jamaica, 1958, by shares of ordinal groups, of income units (family, household, or tax returns)*[2]

Units (%)	0–60	81–90	91–5	96–100
Share (%)	19·5	18	13·3	30·2

top 5 per cent was not particularly high by comparison with other developing countries, but the next 15 per cent of the population did enjoy an unusually high share of the national income, and as a consequence of this factor, Jamaica emerged in an international comparison as being characterized by a remarkably unequal distribution of income. Indeed, 'Jamaica has about the most unequal distribution recorded'.[3] Later studies, based on slightly different sources, broadly confirmed these findings, and showed that the relative distribution of income remained stable at least as late as 1965.[4] There is no reason to assume that there have been fundamental changes since.

There is a temptation to rewrite this distribution in terms of a simple class model. However, these figures also reflect, perhaps with equal weight, the differential rewards available to workers in different sectors of the economy; and in particular, between workers in agriculture and others. Using the 1960 figures, it was calculated that agricultural workers earned 35 per cent of the average per capita product; workers in manufacturing industry and private services earned about the average; while workers in construction, public utilities, transportation and distribution earned much more than the average. Workers in the mining industry earned over four times the average.[5] As one authority summed the matter up, 'Much of the poverty in Jamaica is the consequence of the low productivity in agriculture'.[6] The dimensions of inequality in Jamaica are not only horizontal but also lateral, between town and country. Within the towns, one can also identify particular slum areas which, like many rural districts, are virtually outside the economy of modern Jamaica. The educational opportunities, central to possibilities of social mobility, reflect both of these differences, and exacerbate them.

The control of the major capital resources is highly concentrated, and I have already cited figures which reflect the extent

35

to which control is vested in foreign companies. But Jamaica has its own concentrations of capital, for some of the sugar fortunes remained in the country, and commerce has always been largely in local hands. More recently, some of this money has gone into mining ventures other than bauxite, and into industry, tourism and construction. Fortunes have been made in housing speculations which took advantage of the new demands of the urban employed.

The relationship between Jamaican capitalists and the 'multi-nationals' (mostly based in North America) has not been close, and while leading members of the Jamaican business community have been drawn into the two-party rivalry, on both sides, the foreign concerns have generally been forced to apply indirect diplomatic pressure. There is no necessary identity of interests between local and foreign business interests, and the recent government démarche against the bauxite companies enjoyed the support even of the *Daily Gleaner*, a powerful defender of 'free enterprise'.

The political parties are not simply subservient to capital interests, although they and the unions are concerned to increase private investment in the interest of increasing employment. Together with the unions they have also occasionally restricted the uncontrolled use of great capital power, and successive governments have built up their own direct economic power, both through direct holdings in industries and in the capacity to legislate controls, grant licences, etc. The previous government bought up most of the sugar estates in foreign hands (with the enthusiastic co-operation of the companies involved). More recently, shares have been taken in other concerns and are now being demanded in the bauxite companies; and huge government investments in petroleum refining and the processing of alumina have been mooted.

Characteristically in developing countries, such a situation opens the way to widespread corruption of politicians, civil servants and trade unionists, who are bought out by foreign and local businessmen. This has happened only intermittently in Jamaica, and never on a great scale. The power of the government in the economy has not been seriously undermined.[7] The future power of the government is enhanced by the new bargaining strength of primary producers, and while bauxite and sugar are not to be equated with oil, they are still in short supply, and the

Jamaican government has been actively pursuing the formation of producer country bargaining groups. Thus the future economic development of Jamaica is not at the mercy of the economic considerations of great capitalists. In particular, the future of Jamaica's agriculture is very largely in the hands of the government.

The following chapters discuss the social structure of contemporary Jamaica. I then go on to describe the political system. Economy, polity and social relationships are integrally connected; but each has a life of its own, and changes in one sphere of organization have often unpredictable effects on the others. Money does not simply equal power, nor even high status; and the relationship between social position and political influence is complicated. This is particularly true at times of rapid social change.

Part two

Social Structure and Social Change

Chapter 7

Social Structure and Social Change

In a modern society, particularly in a country like Jamaica, people are very conscious of the changes that have occurred in their own lifetime; they point to the symptoms, ponder their own experiences, pass moral and political judgments. Just as they build home-made 'models' of their society, which serve a variety of purposes, so they create folk-sociologies of change. If challenged, they can point to concrete events—our attitudes have changed, our circumstances—compare us to our parents; look at the way in which the new rich act today; look at the rudeness in the streets.

The sociologist therefore is trying to describe something which is real, experienced, to the members of the society; and which can be measured in various objective ways—demographically, by economic statistics, etc. The problem, however, is to develop a model of social structure which will encompass both the objective indices and at some level the folk models; but which will do more. A sociological model must also explain, which means that it must show how a variety of different bits of reported experience, observed social behaviour, statistical data, fit together. The problem in analysing social change is no different, simply more complicated.

My problem here is to conceptualize the social structure of contemporary Jamaica in relation to its economic and political organization; and to indicate the ways in which it has been changing. The enterprise is not as hopeless as it may seem, for the 1950s saw a series of studies of the same kind, undertaken mainly by Jamaican sociologists; and historians have attempted similar analyses for earlier periods of Jamaican history. These analyses vary in many ways, but have a common basic set of assumptions. In brief, they assume that Jamaican social structure

41

has always been best understood in terms of a model of social stratification, in which 'race' and 'class' interact to define distinct interest groups, or strata, or even, perhaps, sub-societies, which form the units of the total system. Where detailed studies of local communities have been made, these have concentrated either on the social relations of lower-class neighbours, or on the investigation of some feature believed to characterize lower-class social life. (The assumption has been that the middle-class aspired to, and the upper-class achieved, 'normal' Western European modes of life.)

My own analysis depends on the rejection of most of these assumptions. I do not believe that there are clearly-defined strata or classes in Jamaica; I do not believe that social relations within any one 'level' of society or any locale can be understood in isolation; and above all, I do not believe that the folk-models of Jamaicans—which, as I shall show, provide the common units of analysis, and define the problems which have been investigated in detail—can serve as a starting-point for the understanding of Jamaican society. I hope that the issues will emerge clearly as the analysis proceeds, but perhaps it will be useful to discuss theoretically one of the crucial issues, in order to make my own position more explicit.

For the sociologist, stratification means a system of groupings, hierarchically ordered, and with differential access to wealth, status, and power. What kind of groupings are involved? In some cases there may be legally defined categories, or highly self-conscious groups, perhaps marked unambiguously by 'racial' features, by a distinctive language, or by region. Alternatively, at the other extreme, the groupings may be no more than clusters of individuals defined only by the sociologist using some criteria which he considers significant, but lacking either external definition or self-consciousness. Hindu castes are a classic example of the former type, while the categories of a census (for example, the Registrar-General's categories in Britain) are often examples of the latter type, sociological constructs without politico-jural status or a sense of identity.

However, there is a problem here. People everywhere habitually formulate 'we/they' categories, dividing up the people with whom they come into contact, or know about, into situationally variable clusters of 'people like us' and the rest. While such categories are ego-centred and situationally generated, they may link up with more stable conceptions of their society being made up of groups conforming to such we/they discriminations. This may be a function of a number of factors—descent, economic circumstances, language, culture, religion, or residence. Such categories, even when widely shared, are in the end particularistic models of the society made from the vantage point of a particular set of people. Other members of the same society, differently situated, may tend to carve their society up into different we/they categories. To take a simple and simplified example—members of a middle-class may perceive of their society as being divided into three strata; while members of the upper and lower classes (in a very simplistically conceived society) may operate more naturally in terms of a two-class model. This example suggests two further considerations. First of all, it may be that all the members of a society speak a single cultural language of stratification (defined by the shared notion of 'class'), while using it to create different models. If the basic language of the folk-models varies, one is probably dealing with two sub-societies. Second, the example makes sense only if the models of variously situated actors are explained against the background of an objective model constructed by an outsider—otherwise, of course, one could not identify *who* is favouring model one as against model two.

Thus any model of stratification must include, but distinguish, actors' models and objective definitions of strata; and the latter may be based on legal, cultural, economic or regional criteria. Such models may be closely related, and the variations between actors' models may be limited, although infused with different judgments of the total society. This is almost certain to be true where members of a society are ranked by law, for example by differential rights to citizenship based on 'race'. In South Africa (to take an extreme example), the population is divided by law into discrete segments on the basis of 'race', and each racial segment is granted differential political rights, and differential access to economic, educational, recreational and residential opportunities. In such a situation, too, there is a tendency—reinforced by official policy—for the various standard measures of stratification to coincide. Access to power, wealth, prestige, etc. is crucially affected by 'racial' status. Obviously, the actors' models embody these 'racial' categories as their fundamental units, and a sociologist would be ill-advised to attempt an analysis of the situation without granting such units prime importance. This does not mean that the sociologists' model would coincide with such actors' models, or be in precisely the same language— they must include factors which may have vital importance in prefiguring change, or which may be suppressed by the obsession with race, but nevertheless influence social relations in a demonstrable fashion.[1]

Most modern societies do not present such rigid, externally-defined strata, and both the actors and the observer must find their units of analysis for themselves. The actor may well employ stratification models which stress principles of discrimination which a sociologist might consider unhelpful, or even misleading, for his particular purposes—as demanding explanation themselves, rather than as providing guides to the understanding of the society. A Marxist sociologist, for example, will attempt to identify the 'real' classes, defined in terms of objective relationships of production. He will not expect these classes to be self-conscious. Indeed, he will expect the mystifications of the ruling class to obscure their existence until through a dialectical process the deprived class develops self-consciousness, and the 'true' nature of the underlying social conflict emerges. The 'class in itself' is brought through a series of confrontations to a realization of its common interests and becomes a 'class for itself'.

The Marxist model is perhaps the boldest assertion of the existence of latent but crucial groups in a hierarchy, despite the absence of explicit confirmation in actors' models. However, the problem presents itself, in a weaker form perhaps, to any sociologist concerned with stratification. All sociologists expect certain shared, objective circumstances to produce repetitive patterns of choices for people similarly situated, even if they are more or less unaware of their shared situation. For example, in Britain the Liberal party is most consistently successful in traditional and isolated agricultural areas—North Devon, remote parts of Scotland, etc. This is explicable, even in the absence of any sense of identity between a North Devon villager and an islander off the Scottish coast.

However, the issues are never easy to resolve, for modern societies are characteristically in a state of flux, and there is seldom more than a very rough correlation between wealth, power, and prestige. Moreover, different indices of status may be differently weighted in different situations, or by differently placed individuals. Thus actors in most modern societies rely on several models of social stratification, and vary their reliance upon them according to circumstance; and the sociologist can use a one-dimensional model only for very specific and limited purposes.

These are broad considerations and gross contrasts. My point is that in trying to understand and conceptualize Jamaican social structure and social change I have moved away from the classical analyses of Jamaica, both in questioning the usefulness of looking for definite and unvarying gross stratified categories of people as a starting point; and, even more fundamentally, in my attitude to Jamaican folk-models. The classical Jamaican analyses have looked at Jamaica as (roughly) a variant of the South African kind of society.

Jamaica under slavery was a society in which the various dimensions of stratification coincided very closely, because of external political definition; and the actors' models presumably reflected these realities fairly accurately. Jamaica today is most certainly not a society of this type. This is obvious enough, but a number of Jamaican historians and sociologists have argued as if the categories laid down under slavery (or, perhaps, as modified in the immediate post-emancipation period) are still objectively clearly defined, along all relevant dimensions, and still provide the actors with their basic categories. These assumptions are clearly built into most of the models of Jamaican sociologists as recently as the 1950s. If, as is evident, modern Jamaica does not yield to an analysis in such terms, one can choose between two options. Either there has been a complete transformation in one generation—we are now in a state of transition after centuries of stability. Or, alternatively, the analyses of Jamaica published in the immediate post-war period must be recast. No doubt the truth lies in between; but where?

Chapter 8

Orthodox Models and the Traditional System —the Nineteenth Century

In presenting the issue in the previous chapter I was perhaps unjustly sweeping in my characterizations of Jamaican studies. In this chapter I hope to redress the balance, for I examine the social development of Jamaica, however briefly, in terms of the major specific studies of social history and social structure, particularly the studies made in the immediate post-war period.

Professor M. G. Smith has published an influential analysis of the British West Indies in about 1820, which serves as a useful starting point.[1] He distinguished

> three main social sections defined primarily by legal status, as free with full civil rights, free with limited civil rights, and unfree

and showed that these sections

> were composed in the main, but not universally, of persons who differed also in race and colour. Thus the whites were all free but were internally differentiated, free persons with limited civil rights were in the main coloured, but included some black, and the unfree were predominantly black but included some coloured persons. Thus, though racial elements were of great prominence in the historical development of these social sections, at this period the two were not homologous.

The blacks were, of course, the slaves recruited from Africa; the whites were the British masters and their followers. The free coloured people were either slaves who had been manumitted or more commonly the children of master-slave liaisons, who had been granted special status. Smith emphasized the institutional and cultural distinctions between these sections, so that in his analysis each became virtually a sub-society, each with its own way of life, related in a structure of domination. Moreover, this structure survived its original economic rationality and was maintained as long as possible, despite heavy economic costs, because of its social benefits for the ruling section.

Part of the importance of Smith's analysis is that it provides the basis for his analysis of modern Caribbean societies,[2] and as the 'plural society' model of Jamaica it has influenced most modern studies.

One of the problems with this approach is that even for the early nineteenth century, it seems to brush aside the obvious alliances and shared interests of the ruling class and the 'free coloured' population. Professor Broom, who shares substantially the same approach, referred to James Stewart's report (published in 1823) that by the early nineteenth century 95 per cent of the white men had coloured mistresses, and that their children were inheriting substantial amounts of property; although he criticizes Stewart (no doubt correctly) for exaggeration.[3] But the tendency was clear enough, and the white legislature often tried, and failed, to check it. What, one wonders, would Smith make of the case cited by 'Monk' Lewis, of the slave-owner brought to trial for murdering a slave?[4]

His mistress was the coroner's natural daughter, and the coroner himself was similarly connected with the custos of Clarendon. In consequence of this family compact, no inquest was held, no enquiry was made; the whole business was allowed to be slurred over.

All the 'family' connections were, of course, via coloured women and children.

The 'free coloured' were all subject to legal restrictions until the 1830s, but even before the emancipation of the slaves some had achieved considerable social status. In 1826 freemen of colour claimed to own about 50,000 slaves,[5] and Dr Braithwaite cites as an example of the rich coloureds the case of James Swaby, a mulatto whose (white) father left him two large estates in 1826 and who owned over 200 slaves. 'He had also been to Charter-

house and held a commission as a lieutenant in the British army.'
Writing of the immediate pre-emancipation situation, Professor
Curtin leaves no doubt of the bonds linking white and coloured:[6]

> In spite of social barriers, the brown people were very close
> to the attitudes and general outlook on the world of their
> white neighbours, at least in the sense that some coloured
> people were found holding every shade of opinion found
> among members of the white class. The people of colour
> were very conscious of their European heritage and
> extremely proud of it. . . . They discriminated socially
> against the darker members of their own class, they were
> just as prejudiced as the whites in their relations with
> Negro slaves, and finally a minority of the coloured group
> joined the whites in the fight against emancipation.

The period 1830–65 witnessed the political incorporation of
the more prosperous members of the old 'freeman' category,
and saw them, together with the old ruling class, battling over
their relationship to Britain and trying to come to terms with the
new position of the former slaves. The old ruling class resented
the comparatively liberal demands of Britain, while the new men
from the former freeman class trusted the British, on the whole,
more than they did the traditicnal ruling-class. In both groups,
however, there were various shades of opinion, and on the whole
they were united in their fear of 'a Haiti' in Jamaica, and thus
generally agreed upon the necessity of withholding political power
from the mass of recently freed slaves. The period ended with the
riots at Morant Bay, where some coloured parliamentarians sided
with the black mob, while others supported the Governor and
leading planters in their bloody repression. In the end Jamaica's
leaders agreed to hand over power to Britain, on the argument
that 'Parliament will always control the Ministry, and will never
allow the island to be placed in the hands of those who have no
property rights.'[7]

There is no question but that during this period the boundaries
between the white ruling section and the middle coloured and
black section of Smith's description were considerably shifted, if
not displaced. John Bigelow, an American visitor to Jamaica, wrote
in the mid-nineteenth century that[8]

one accustomed to the proscribed condition of the free
black in the United States, will constantly be startled at
the diminished importance attached here to the matter of
complexion. Intermarriages are constantly occurring between
the white and coloured people, their families associate
together within the ranks to which by wealth and colour
they respectively belong, and public opinion does not
recognize any social distinctions based exclusively on
colour. Of course, cultivated or fashionable people will not
receive coloured persons of inferior culture and wordly
resources, but the rule of discrimination is scarcely more
rigorous against those than against whites. They are
received at the 'King's House' . . . and they are invited to
(the governor's) table with fastidious courtesy. The wife
of the present mayor of Kingston is a 'brown' woman . . .
so also is the wife of the Receiver General himself, an
English gentleman, and one of the most exalted public
functionaries upon the island. . . . One unacquainted with
the extent to which the amalgamation of races has gone
here, is constantly liable to drop remarks in the presence
of white persons, which, in consequence of the mixture of
blood that may take place in some branch of their families,
are likely to be very offensive. I was only protected from
frequent *contretemps* of this kind, by the timely caution of a
lady, who in explaining its propriety, said that unless one
knows the whole collateral kindred of a family in Jamaica,
he is not safe in assuming that they have not some coloured
connections.

By the late 1830s, too, all legal distinctions based on colour had
been removed.

This is not to say that there were not considerable cultural
variations between ex-slaves and former masters, let alone vast
material disparities; nor that racial discrimination was not central
to the definition of social status. However, the lines were growing
fuzzier. Even the slaves cannot be said to have retained a distinctive culture into the nineteenth century; the disappearance of
African languages is a good index of this. The distinction made
by slaves between the Africa-born and the more prestigious
creole slaves, a distinction recognized by whites, is another index.

49

A devoted attempt to define a distinctive Jamaican slave culture, by a historian who believes in its continued political relevance, yielded only a handful of 'customs' and songs.[9]

If 'cultural' differences are difficult to pin down, and political and social divisions were not rigid, at least between whites and prosperous coloured people, then what was left of Smith's 'three social sections' when their legal definition was abandoned? Summing up the period leading up to the Morant Bay rebellion and the failure of self-government, Curtin writes:[10]

> Hiding behind every aspect of the failure to attain the cultural and social assimilation of the *two Jamaicas* was the background of racial distinctions and racial consciousness. The question of race was beneath the surface of every Jamaican problem, intermingling with other issues and making all solutions more difficult. . . . *The threefold racial division* helped to ease tensions somewhat—racial, as opposed to class, lines were never as tightly drawn in Jamaica as in the southern United States. In Jamaica the race question was often hidden behind other issues, while in the American South other issues tended to hide behind racial conflict. (My emphasis.)

His two Jamaicas are 'European' and 'African' Jamaica, but they cannot be rigidly separated because of the existence of the ambiguous middle category; and the 'threefold racial division' is again not a threefold social division, but rather a three-tier model of race used by many Jamaicans, and, as he says, a model which cross-cut the lines between his 'two Jamaicas'. Smith and Curtin agree that Jamaica was fundamentally segmented in hierarchical sections; but they disagree about the very number of the sections, and their criteria—law, colour, culture, politics—cross-cut even their own divisions.

We know little about the period of Crown Colony rule (1866–1944). These were obviously years of major social, economic and, by definition, political change; but historians of Jamaica have neglected the period. The image of Jamaica one gets from reading scholarly work is one of a country which emerged from slavery, failed to reorganize itself, and then somehow just lapsed until the workers rioted in the 1930s, and the middle-class became nationalistic in the 1940s. I believe that this hiatus in our know-ledge is both cause and effect of the domination of the model of Jamaica being made up of discrete racial/cultural sections defined in a slave society. The post-war sociologists 'read' the new Jamaica in terms of the anti-society of slavery; this was both their model and their standard of judgment, and the judgment was stern.

Chapter 9

The Last Generation

A number of anthropological field-studies were carried out in Jamaica in the late 1940s and early 1950s, by Edith Clarke, Fernando Henriques, and M. G. Smith, all Jamaicans, and by the social psychologist Madeline Kerr. There were also some more limited studies carried out by American sociologists. Rich in descriptive data, and infused with more or less fully-developed views of the nature of the total Jamaican society, they provide, together, an extremely useful picture of Jamaica a generation ago.

Although the descriptive materials in these accounts tend to support each other, the various studies adopt different theoretical positions. Nevertheless, the common theoretical assumptions can, today, be recognized too; and they are perhaps of even greater significance than the differences, although the differences were sometimes pursued with polemical violence. Like the American sociologist, Leonard Broom, these scholars all worked from the basic assumption that Jamaica was divided into a set of stratified sections, defined largely but not entirely by race, and deriving from the organization of the slave society. They differed mainly on the way in which such diverse groups were integrated. The key issue was whether cultural values provided the basis for cohesion, or whether culture and values differed between sections, so exacerbating the potential for conflict, with the consequence that the societies continued in their old forms through the monopoly of force in the hands of one racial/cultural section. This debate was not restricted to the sociology of Jamaica: it became the central issue in the sociology of the British West Indies. Henriques, Brathwaite and Raymond T. Smith lined up on one side of the argument, and M. G. Smith, Leo Despres, David Lowenthal and others on the contrary side—Parsonians *v.* plural society theorists. My argument is that the fundamental assumptions shared by both parties cannot be sustained, and that therefore the debate is a dead-end.

A brief consideration of the approaches of M. G. Smith and Fernando Henriques will serve to illustrate my argument, and will also bring out the central descriptive features of the studies. Both argued that Jamaica was divided into three strata, which Smith described much as he had described the three sections of West Indian societies in the 1820s:[1]

> The three distinctive institutional systems characteristic of
> contemporary Jamaica ... define a society divided into
> three social sections. For initial reference, we may think
> of these sections as the white, the brown and the black,
> this being the order of their current and historical dominance,
> and the exact reverse of their relative numerical strength.
> Although these colour coefficients are primarily heuristic,
> they indicate the racial majority and cultural ancestry of
> each section accurately. The white section which ranks
> highest locally represents the culture of mid-twentieth-
> century West European society. It is the dominant section,
> but also the smallest, and consists principally of persons
> reared abroad from early childhood. The black or lowest
> section may include four-fifths of the population, and
> practices a folk culture containing numerous elements
> reminiscent of African societies and Caribbean slavery.
> The brown intermediate section is culturally and biologically
> the most variable, and practices a general mixture of
> patterns from the higher and lower groups. This mixture
> seems to involve a combination of institutional forms as
> often as institutional syncretism. Thus the culture of the
> middle section includes coexistent institutional alternatives
> drawn from either of the two remaining traditions, as well
> as those forms which are peculiar to itself.

The existence of these three bounded 'social sections' is asserted, and each is identified with a mean racial type, cultural forms, and position in a structure of domination. Smith continued:[2]

> The integration of these three sections within the larger
> society has never been very high; and for cohesion Jamaica

53

has depended mainly on those forms of social control
implicit in the economic system and explicit in government.

It is all very neat—though he does throw in a tantalizing qualification:[3]

> Even so, patterns of interpersonal relations do not always
> correspond with these cultural divisions; and in every cultural
> section there are some persons who habitually associate
> with others who carry a different cultural tradition more
> readily than with those of their own cultural community.
> The fewness of these marginal individuals is no adequate
> guide to their importance.

Henriques also identified three social strata, though he defined
them differently. In his version, Jamaican society was based on a
'colour-class' system. There were three classes, upper, middle,
and lower, and each was again divided by colour into two segments.
The upper class contained higher white and lower fair coloured
sections, while the middle and lower classes were each divided
into superior coloured and inferior black sections. Again, it
seems neat enough, but he immediately slips in descriptive
qualifications. His initial qualification is perhaps the most confusing. This 'colour-class pyramid', while it 'is useful to indicate
economic status . . . does not necessarily indicate social position.
For example a black doctor is not generally accepted as belonging
to the upper class.'[4] His analysis of his own social position brings
out the difficulty of simplifying Jamaican social structure:[5]

> I am Jamaican born but left the island at an early age and
> have only maintained intermittent contact since. My
> parents were both fair coloured people of the upper class,
> my father being a merchant as was his father before him.
> My brothers and sisters are all dark but have European-
> like features and hair. All members of the family rank as
> upper class . . . because of their appearance and the social
> status of my parents. In this instance dark colouring and
> European features leads the lower classes to characterize
> the family as 'coolies'; that is East Indians.

His rich descriptive material brings out very clearly the complex factors which go into status ascription in Jamaica, and again and again undermine the utility of his neat 'colour-class pyramid'. For example, dealing with the anomalous black men of high status, he remarks:[6]

> Extreme wealth on the part of the black man, in itself
> comparatively rare, will lead to a greater degree of
> acceptance (by members of the élite). Of much greater
> advantage is the possession of a fair or white wife. . . .
> But the acceptance achieved by whatever means will never
> be the same as that extended to fair people of similar
> economic position.

Here the definition of the upper-class is largely a matter of the self-definition of an élite group in a provincial town. This is not sufficient to characterize a social system, for judgments of status vary from group to group. His descriptions emphasize ambiguities and variations, but in argument he retreats to his rigid and simplistic model. While this model resembles Smith's in some ways, his conclusion is diametrically opposed. Jamaica is not torn apart by divergent values and held together by force. On the contrary, the society exemplifies the power of a 'white bias' which everyone accepts as natural. Post-war Jamaica was 'a society where the majority of the population is coloured and black and is held, partly by its own consent, in a purely social subjection by a white and fair group'.[7]

While Henriques, Smith and others argued that at least until the 1950s Jamaica was made up of three racial/cultural/social strata, they defined these rather differently and multiplied descriptive qualifications. Others favoured different definitions of the number of strata. Thus Madeline Kerr worked with a two-tier model, and argued that 'Most [Jamaicans] are of mixed origin',[8] and Curtin posited for the nineteenth century a similar two-tier model, but modified, and made more flexible, rather in the Henriques manner, by a three-tier racial division.[9] Most argued that these strata originated in the eighteenth century and persisted with minor modifications after the emancipation of the slaves and the changes in legal status of the subject population.

55

I have already rasied some questions with respect to these kinds of models. For one thing, the developments in the nineteenth century did not simply reinforce or perpetuate colour-classes or social sections. Intermarriage, inheritance and succession across colour lines, civil rights defined by property alone—all these factors were clearly generating a different series of social distinctions from those which had been legally entrenched (though often breached) in the slave society. Another problem is one of methodology. What these scholars have done, in my view, is to translate into more rigid sociological language various folk-models, and so they fail to ask to what extent their 'sections' are simply sociological constructs, and to what extent they are self-conscious groups. They are simply accepted, facts of nature, which need only be clearly defined (a task in which, symptomatically, they all fail). By confusing the status of actors' and observers' models, many of these sociologists and social historians have imposed a misleadingly clear-cut and also falsely timeless value upon their variables—'colour' or 'race', 'culture' and 'class'. These terms correspond closely to Jamaican folk-concepts, but while Jamaicans maximize their ambiguity, the social scientist strains to attain precision, and is lost.

Consider the Jamaican notion of 'colour' ('race', 'complexion'). Henriques sketched it very accurately:[10]

'Colour' is evaluated in terms of actual colour, hair formation, features, and skin texture. . . . In Jamaica in order to classify an individual according to colour all the characteristics have to be assessed. It so happens that the majority of the fair coloured have a fair complexion and European hair and features so that their classification is simple. But as regards others it becomes a very complex matter. For instance a person might exhibit European-like features, but his hair might be more negroid than European. In such a case his colour status in the society would be determined by the texture of his skin. This individual would rank above a person of similar complexion with 'good' hair, but whose features were more African. A dark person with 'good' hair and features ranks above a fair person with 'bad' hair and features. There are a very large number of such combinations.

And a footnote explains that 'good' denotes European, 'bad' African.

Not only do the variety of criteria permit a variety of classifications, but the situation is further confused by the fact that prestige may modify colour classification. Nor is this a novel phenomenon. One of the first students of the Jamaican dialect wrote, in 1868, glossing the traditional black term for a white man ('Backra'):[11]

> it is not used exclusively in referring to the white man, a brown or black gentleman is also called so in acknowledgement of his gentility or genteel appearance; but this little privilege is only given him with his good morning or good evening, or when he is asked a favour, otherwise he is only 'gentleman' or 'smart fella'. Should he however by his education and position, or money, move much in the upper · class society, then he is said to turn 'pure-pure backra'.

Madeline Kerr, concerned with the psychological difficulties, the crises of identity, which she encountered among many Jamaicans, suggested that one even finds[12]

> different personality constellations producing what appear to be different attitudes to colour in the same person. One day a person will be bitter and anti-white, yet when another constellation is involved he will be concerned with fears and dislike only of people darker than himself. It is as if in some constellations he is the almost white man with white ideals, in others he is the dark man resenting white domination. These constellations exist together and to some extent neutralize each other, leaving the individual perplexed and insecure.

These ambiguities do not imply that the underlying folk notions of race are obscure. On the contrary, all these ideas derive from the classical Western view that human beings are biologically sorted into discrete 'races' (above all, the white and black), and that 'racial differences' are reflected not only in physical appearance but also in ways of behaving, which are believed to be equally determined genetically, and equally distinctive. Thus in Jamaica,

the ideal notion of 'white' and 'black' races has always gone together with ideal notions of the associated cultures of 'England'
and 'Africa'. The historian Elsa Goveia pointed out that in the
debate on emancipation all parties used a 'pseudo-Africa' as
their point of reference;[13] the 'England' of the Jamaican model is
no less a 'pseudo-England', an idealized abstraction, which, like
the other basic notions of race, is scarcely amenable to modification
as a consequence of direct observation or experience. The folk-
model is therefore based on a dichotomy, which is believed to be
natural and unalterable—on the one side, white, English, master;
on the other, black, African, slave. People of mixed ancestry are
in the middle, deriving traits from both racial sources. A two- or
three-tier model of race/culture/class serves to operationalize
this basic paradigm, depending on the position of the actor
himself.

To the outsider, the cultural uniformity of Jamaica is very
striking, but there are at the extremes two identifiable and prominent groups of people who serve to give the model potency.
On the one hand, the former plantocrats, now represented by a
few members of the decaying aristocracy, some expatriates, and
a few snobbish Jamaicans, to whom (in certain moods at any rate)
the old order is very real. At the other end are the Rastafarians,
slum-dwellers who make a cult of the idea of a millenarian return
to Africa, to whom African-ness is all. In a column which has
become justly famous, a Jamaican journalist described this old
upper crust as the 'white Rastas' of suburban St Andrew. He
wrote:[14]

> The West Kingston Rastafarians refuse to work for Babylon,
> think of themselves as the chosen people, regard their
> repatriation to Africa as a matter of right, and hold the
> King of Ethiopia to be a god. The St Andrew Rastafarians
> refuse to work for anyone but their own kind, think of
> themselves as being of a different calibre, as well as of
> a different and superior race, regard England as their
> spiritual home, and hold the throne of England in the
> reverence befitting the Divine Right of Kings. There really
> isn't much difference between them and their West Kingston
> brothers, except that they smell better. Yet the horror with
> which they regard the Rastafarians of the slums is equalled

only by the horror with which the Rastafarians of the slums regard them. It is a very great pity. The two groups are the only people who can be said to share a common culture. I think it is only the use of soap that stands between them. And the use of ganja (marijuana) in moderation rather than the use of whisky, often to excess, for the St Andrew Rastafarian is too often an alcoholic.

The majority of Jamaicans do not exist on a sort of continuum between these strange positions; they regard themselves as the ordinary Jamaicans, and many will define themselves as members of the 'middle-class', that most elastic of Jamaican folk categories.[15]

If Jamaican folk-models derive from a single basic notion of 'race', it should nevertheless be quite clear that this notion is in operation crucially ambiguous, and ill-adapted to the definition of sharp social boundaries. It should be apparent, none the less, that the sociological models which do assert the existence of such boundaries draw their variables from these folk-notions, and give them a spurious clarity and classificatory power. The difficulty of drawing such objective boundaries is clearly demonstrated by another sociological study from this period, a study made by an American sociologist of a small town in Jamaica.

Professor Taylor followed the then common American socio-logical technique of defining social strata: he asked a sample of people to rank various members of the community, and then attempted to abstract the criteria they had used, and to define the boundaries. He came up with 22 terms of colour designation alone, and found that even with this obsessional interest, designa-tions and classifications varied. However, he abstracted five classes, but found that even then the criteria of status were not uniform. His class of small cultivators with economic sidelines was most concerned with colour—'After a lower prestige-grade mother had ended her confinement, her friends enquired about a child's colour before ascertaining its sex.' In the upper group (minor professionals and traders) the key status-symbol was the avoidance of manual labour. 'A teacher could not dust a book, nor could a housewife carry a parcel from an automobile or enter her kitchen unless to supervise'; but he observed that darker individuals in this category had to worry more about maintaining appearances.[16] A similar study in another small town found that 'Status symbols

... were complex, ambiguous, and not necessarily monopolized by people from one prestige level.'[17]

It is evident then that Jamaicans use various criteria in ranking themselves and others. Today occupation (usually related to education) is the dominant criterion, but as in the past—though with different weight—many Jamaicans also evaluate 'colour', style, modes of consumption, etc. to yield a complex and flexible series of social classifications. These criteria are not necessarily congruent with each other, and most are ambiguously defined, so that they do not yield rigid categories and ascriptions. On the other hand, they all derive their power from their ultimate reference to the underlying notion that 'race' is a fact of nature, dividing human beings into obvious and distinct and unequal sets, and that 'race' involves not merely appearance but also habits, customs, beliefs, and potential. Jamaican sociologists have generally taken these underlying ideas and refined them, made them extremely clear and definite, and so have emerged with the notion that Jamaica is in fact made up of rigidly formed sections defined by the congruence of criteria of race, culture and class. This is a fundamental error. The whole point of the Jamaican notions is that they are *not* rigid, although they refer back to the idea of a natural and hierarchical social order.

My difference with the classical Jamaican sociologists is therefore quite simple. They have taken rigid legal models, infused with ideas of natural racial distinctions which were established in Jamaica in the eighteenth and nineteenth centuries. From these sources they have created misleading and timeless models of what is in action a far from rigid or rigidly perceived social system. My emphasis is precisely on the variability and ambiguity of modern criteria of status, and on the variety of ascriptions they can yield. Indeed, they can be made to yield a number of distinct folk-models, all using the same terms, but all drawing attention to different aspects of the social reality. Most Jamaican models stress race, but they vary from an American-style 'black *v.* white' model through the classical 'black/brown/white' model to a multiracial 'one nation' model, which is today the one preferred in public by the establishment. Other versions stress education, opposing the illiterate and the reasonable. (This has some neo-racist elements at times—as in the view that the bulk of the population suffers from brain damage as a result of malnutrition in early childhood, and therefore cannot benefit from education.) Others employ moral values, or occupational categories or relative wealth to yield other models, all situationally relevant, all occasionally useful and even comforting, but none being exclusively preferred or dominant at all times.

In my views these ambiguities and variations are of the essence. It is in part because these models are so flexible in practice that there is less group consciousness and conflict than might be expected on the basis of the history of racial discrimination and the current gross inequalities of wealth and opportunity. Neat stratification models of Jamaica tell one little about the social realities, and such approaches have inevitably led to the sterile debate about how the society coheres—whether such disparate 'groups' or 'classes' or 'social sections' are held together through consensus or the use of force. If one takes seriously the lack of consistency between the various possible objective scales and the various subjective measures (among themselves, and with reference to each other) one is led rather to understand how in this extremely complex situation people refer to different sets or values in different situations; and do not agree on firm social boundaries; and are not therefore consistently (in their own view) members of self-conscious and ranked categories. It is meaningless to argue about how the ranked groups cohere in a society, because for the actors there are no clearly demarcated groups which are consistently ranged in positions of opposition or mutual support. It may be that racial or economic conflict groups will emerge in the future. I shall argue later that it is more likely that the present rather fluid situation will not yield to a process of polarization.

Chapter 10

Race and Class — Objective Indices

In some sense, the Jamaican notions which I have summed up in terms of 'race', 'class' and 'culture' do correspond to facets of the social reality which a foreign observer, ignorant of Jamaican social constructs, might identify and feel to be important. That is, they have an objective correlate—although, I would argue, it is dangerous to distinguish too completely a set of 'objective facts' from either the sociological theory or the folk-sociology which defines and almost creates them. In this chapter I attempt to formulate some 'objective' statements of these variables and their interrelationships.

Racial classifications pose a peculiar problem, since while certain phenotypical features are a good guide to elements of 'racial' ancestry, they are subject to considerable variation, particularly in a country where different stocks have interbred for centuries. Laymen are much more certain than scientists about the clear boundaries of 'races', and their specific characteristics—indeed, scientists have largely abandoned the idea that it is useful to define any racial groupings within the general category, modern man. Moreover, the Jamaican ambiguities in the definitions of racial features, discussed in the previous chapter, have naturally affected census figures. Noting that 'census shifts underscore the ambiguity of West Indian colour classification', Professor Lowenthal pointed out that:[1]

between 1943 and 1960 the 'coloured' proportion of Kingston declined from 33 to 14 per cent. The explanation lies in nomenclature as well as in-migration; dark-skinned Kingstonians were less content to be labelled 'black' in 1943 than 'African' in 1960.

None the less, Jamaican censuses have for many years attempted to classify the population by race, and the returrs give some idea of the proportion of people who appear to be of African and European ancestry. In 1960 the enumerators were instructed to enter the racial classification volunteered by respondents, who were presented with a choice between nine possible categories, including one which was labelled 'other'.

TABLE 6   *Percentage racial origin of Jamaican population according to censuses, 1881–1960*[2]

Census year	Afro-African	European	Afro-European	Chinese, Afro-Chinese	East Indian, Afro-East Indian	Other races	Not stated
1881	76·5	18·9	2·5	0·0	1·9	..	0·2
1891	76·4	19·1	2·3	0·1	1·6	..	0·5
1911	75·8	19·6	1·9	0·3	2·1	..	0·3
1921	77·0	18·3	1·7	0·4	2·2	..	0·4
1943	78·1	17·5	1·1	1·0	2·1	0·2	..
1960	76·3	15·1	0·8	1·2	3·4	3·2	..

Over the past century, the tiny European part of the population has been declining proportionately to the whole, the African proportion has remained stable, constituting about three-quarters of the population, and the various 'mixed race' categories have become progressively more significant. The rapid growth of the categories 'Chinese, Afro-Chinese' and 'East Indian, Afro-East Indian' is attributable mainly to an increase in the number of people of mixed ancestry, and the rise in the category 'others' represents a growing proportion of people whose ancestry defies the enumerators' categories.[3]

For nearly a century and a half such 'racial' identifications have had no legal implications, but do they correspond none the less to social or cultural or economic groupings of some kind? One must first of all distinguish the ethnic enclaves in Jamaica— the East Indians, Chinese and Syrians who arrived in the nineteenth century, and the Jews, who though they were among the first settlers of the island retained a distinct ethnic identity. These ethnic groups each began with distinctive languages, religions, occupations and ties to other countries, and in each case, to varying degrees, such identities persist, and are reflected in special communal organizations. However, they are not ghetto cultures: the creolization of culture and the integration of social relationships have marked them all. The Chinese remain perhaps the closest to a distinct, identified and organized community, and they are concentrated in the retail trade, particularly in groceries; but even they would be regarded as highly assimilated by their counterparts in San Francisco. For the rest, the 'racial' categories do not correspond to community organizations or show other features of ethnic identity; with the end of the colonial period the last elements of official and semi-official racial discrimination have disappeared, and although 'race' enters into the definition of social status, as I have shown this is not a simple cause-effect relationship.

None the less, there is a clear, gross correlation between 'race' and social class. Blacks are concentrated at the bottom of the economic and occupational pyramid (though there are poor 'red' people, and the East Indians are often among the poorest Jamaicans), and light-skinned people become more common at the higher levels (though prosperous, well-educated and influential black Jamaicans are no rarity). The correlation can be illustrated easily enough from census statistics, but in order to bring out the problems with such exercises I shall discuss the analysis made of such material by an American sociologist, Leonard Broom, who used them in an attempt to demonstrate a close relationship between colour and ethnicity and social position.[4]

Broom begins with the assertion that 'The basic racial pattern of Jamaica was laid down in the eighteenth century', and he proceeds, in the familiar fashion, with a brief account of the close (though not perfect) correlation between colour and status position in the slave society. He notes the rise of coloured people, and the incidence of social mobility and intermarriage in the nineteenth century, but his stress is upon continuity. Turning to the Jamaica of the 1940s, he then writes:

Social stratification in Jamaica cannot be understood as an uninterrupted continuum of status positions. No matter what empirical criteria are employed, gross discontinuities are to be found. Given the historical forces briefly reviewed, this fact should cause no surprise, but the extreme character of this status cleavage affects all facets of Jamaican society.

He then takes up the Jamaican census data for 1943, and demonstrates that the various racial and ethnic groups occupy distinct levels of advantage whether one examines education, land ownership, wage levels, or various other indices. Thus the incidence of illiteracy for those seven years old and above was: Blacks, 98·6; East Indians, 97·7; Coloured, 88·9; Chinese, 87·5; Syrians, 51·7; Whites, 38·8. A similar series of gaps marked the distribution, in a similar order, of the other means to wealth and high social position.

Of course, these distributions are not unexpected, given the history of differential 'insertion' of various groups into Jamaican society at different periods. The problem is whether the average of a 'racial' category is of particular social significance. None of these racial groups is closed, nor is social mobility blocked by racial origin; and every occupational level in modern Jamaica above the level of labourer is occupied by people of various colours. Nor does Broom argue that even a generation ago social groups were racially bounded. He writes:

> Polite society is dominated by these whites, or more
> accurately, by the white wives of these men. There are also a
> number of cliques of high status centring on the coloured
> professionals, but the town clubs, the yacht club, and the
> country clubs are not racially exclusive. Their member-
> ships, of course, are disproportionately white and light
> coloured as a consequence of the distribution of money,
> education, and occupation. Perhaps in the country parishes
> one or two clubs composed exclusively of creole whites
> might be found, but these are rare survivals of an earlier
> period.

And when Broom comes to consider the composition of élite occupations, where the gross averages can be broken down, he emerges with an argument about the *disproportionate* success of light coloured people, Syrians, Chinese, etc. In fact his classifications change as well, so that he lists the proportions of doctors, lawyers, etc. who are 'white and light', 'olive', 'light brown', 'dark brown', and 'black' as well as Chinese, Indian, Jewish, of Syrian. I am not sure how he developed a measurable category or

65

olive-coloured, as opposed to light or dark brown professionals, but he cannot mean that to be olive in shade is a specific advantage or disadvantage, or implies different social circumstances, as compared with another shade of brown.

Even before the argument itself demonstrates its own absurdity, the difficulties with this approach are apparent. If colour does not in itself necessarily imply either a particular social position or economic potential, then Broom's gross averages say no more than that if your ancestors were poor you will be much less likely to be well-off than another man whose ancestors were rich. The average black is worse-off than the average coloured Jamaican; but then, in England, the average descendant of a mill-hand is no doubt worse-off than the average descendant of a mill-owner. On the other hand, descent from a slave is generally still physically marked, while descent from an English mill-hand is not, and this does mean that potentially the discrepancies may have social implications. Broom does not discuss them, and they cannot be measured from census returns, but they may take two forms. First of all, the expectation may be that if one is rich one is light, if poor, black. Second, people may associate 'race' and 'class' in political mobilization. I have already discussed some of the ways in which 'colour' and other factors interact in the assessment of status. In later chapters I discuss the political potential of the association of race and class. Here, however, I am trying to pin down 'objective' correlations, and for my present purposes it is sufficient to demonstrate that gross correlations between colour and material advantages are present, but of dubious analytical significance.

'Class' has rarely been treated as distinct from status and colour by sociologists concerned with Jamaica, and so a recent attempt to isolate class factors by Dr Stone is of particular interest. He stratified an urban sample on the basis of occupational categories, and argued that 'occupational strata reflect both differences in material affluence as well as non-material status distinctions such as that between manual and non-manual labour'.[5] His findings are sometimes a little odd, for he tried to discover what his various strata thought about the 'upper-class' and 'middle-class', though these terms are very vague in Jamaica. (He found that workers were on the whole moderately against the upper-class, but not against the middle-class!) More interesting was the lack of specific racial attitudes associated with particular occupational levels, and in general the great extent of tolerance, except perhaps for the Chinese. Moreover, all categories tended to divide between the political parties. The only segment which expressed radical and divergent sentiments were the lumpen-proletariat, the hard-core unemployed of Kingston.

On Stone's evidence, there is little 'class-consciousness' in Kingston, and the variation in attitudes between members of different occupational levels appears to be surprisingly small. Stone's neo-Marxist point of view leads him to suggest that the categories of people with shared material interests, and similar positions in the economic structure, will in due course emerge as self-conscious conflict groups. Whatever one may expect to happen at some unspecified time in the future, the present position, according to my reading of his data, is that social class membership (or at least occupational level) does not crucially affect beliefs about the wider society, or attitudes towards it. Nor does it generate a particular consciousness of the nature of economic exploitation in Jamaica, and so common political or organizational responses.

Finally, 'cultural' variations, so much stressed by some authors, do not seem to me to be remarkable, except at the very top and at the very bottom—among the 'Rastafarians' of suburb and slum. These reflect deliberate reactions to the mainstream culture of the island, and I shall discuss the Rastafarians in some detail later. Of course, there are variations in style, use of language, mode of consumption, etc.; and there are important institutional forms open to the more affluent which are closed to the majority of the population. Jamaica is an extremely inegalitarian society in terms of wealth, and this reflects in part the original dispositions in the 'anti-society' of slave Jamaica. But it is going too far to suggest that there are clear-cut bounded groups, or closed categories, marked, among other things, by a distinct culture. This is a problem best examined, perhaps, on a small canvas, and I shall return to it when describing a rural community in which I carried out a field-study.

To sum up the argument of this chapter, I want to cite, and comment upon, a recent eloquent statement by a newspaper columnist. He wrote, in the *Daily News* (21 August 1973):

> There have always been two Jamaicas. The one which has
> been visible—like the tip of an iceberg—has been a
> multiracial bougeois society of about 100,000 people.
> These people have controlled the political, social, economic
> and academic life of the country; they have been articulate
> and influential so they have been generally accepted as
> 'Jamaica'. . . .
> There is another Jamaica—a nation of nearly two million
> people—who are poor, Black and uneducated. A large
> proportion is illiterate. These people have been inarticulate
> and uninfluential. So they have been virtually 'invisible'.
> Like the submerged section of the iceberg they're there,
> but they aren't seen until it is too late.

There is a gross descriptive value in this, but to jump from these
broad oppositions to a prediction that revolutionary change and
the end of 'bourgeois Jamaica' is imminent is to ignore the fact
that these descriptive poles do not correspond to conscious social
groups, organized or open to organization, and to ignore the
social processes which intervene to prevent polarization. This
sort of description (which can be found in the work of many
social scientists) also by-passes the regional variations, particularly
the differences between town and country. Like most professional
urban Jamaicans, the journalists and social scientists concentrate
on the city's problems.

I began by suggesting that 'objective' indices of social dis-
junctions are less realistic than a natural-science orientation might
suggest. Gross averages are meaningless unless the averages
correspond to some conscious social facts; the social structure of
Jamaica cannot be understood except in terms of the conceptions
and responses of real people living in the society. At the same
time, a consideration of these indices serves to heighten awareness
of the inequalities in Jamaican society. There are a variety of
organizations and systems which serve to maintain the present
disposition of opportunities and means, and although these are
to some extent self-generating, they are also open to use and
manipulation. It is at this level that one begins to connect the
power-structure with the form of the society. I shall be devoting
a special section to the political system, but it is appropriate now
to examine the functioning of the educational system. At once a

mode of social mobility and a means of maintaining the present structure; a means of change and a political institution of great conservative force, the educational system reveals a good deal about the reality of Jamaican society.

Chapter 11

The Educational System

Literacy in Jamaica has never been high, and the greatest failure of the contemporary educational system has been in this most basic field. Citing a survey of entrants into junior secondary schools carried out by the Ministry of Education, in September 1970, Professor Smith reported[1]

> that 54 per cent of the pupils moving into the junior
> secondary schools were functionally illiterate; i.e. unable to
> read beyond the grade IV level; and further that 84 per
> cent of the 3,000 students surveyed were incapable of
> reading at their own grade level.

Even this understates the failure of the system, for the Ministry estimated that nearly 11 per cent of children aged between 6 and 14 were not in school at all.

The primary level of the system is patently inadequate (in terms of its stated goals), but it is by far the most important. In 1968–9 nearly 89 per cent of all students in the public sector were in primary schools, only 10 per cent in secondary schools, and 1 per cent in post-secondary institutions. As this distribution suggests, very few Jamaican children are educated beyond the primary level.

The second level is divided into three streams—the academic secondary schools, the technical high schools, and the comparatively recent 'junior secondary' and 'comprehensive' schools, which last are simply a way of prolonging the inadequate mass primary education for a couple of years. (Although few junior secondary and comprehensive schools have yet found a suitable educational approach and goal, they are now entrusted with 40 per cent of the students in the public secondary sector. Most of

them are little more than elaborate deceptions practised upon
the unsuspecting mass of poor and uneducated Jamaicans.) The
academic secondary schools are traditionally the nurturing ground
for Jamaica's managers and professionals, but despite their
selectivity and high status, they are themselves not particularly
successful in traditional educational terms. Of the candidates
entered for the Cambridge GCE O-level examinations in 1972,
nearly 13 per cent failed to pass a single subject, and only 37 per
cent passed in four subjects. In the London GCE A-level examination in 1971, passes in various subjects ranged from a low of
none at all in zoology, to a high of 37·5 per cent in religious
knowledge. [2]

The tertiary sector is relatively extremely expensive, costing
nearly half as much as infant and primary education, while
catering for just over a hundredth the number of people. It is
geared to the production of a specialized elite, but any rationale
for this policy is undermined by the high rate of professional
emigration. A recent survey showed that 46 per cent of Jamaican
men students at the university and 49 per cent of those at the
technical college were planning to go abroad at graduation, at
least temporarily. [3]

The educational system is, rationally judged, ineffective; but
it does reflect and perpetuate the balance of advantages within
the population. A rough occupational classification might well
oppose the wealthy business and professional people, the salariat,
skilled workers, unskilled urban workers, and the smallholders
and rural labourers. The main divisions would be between unskilled urban workers, smallholders and rural labourers, and the
rest. The educational system is adjusted to this structure. It is
divided into two streams, the main stream embracing the government's primary and all-age schools and the junior secondary,
comprehensive, technical and vocational schools. This copes with
the vast majority of Jamaica's children, and has its own further
education sector, made up of the teacher training colleges and the
technical college. The other sub-system is highly selective. At its
base are the private preparatory schools, which feed the academic
secondary schools. Its successful products go on to the university.
The teacher training colleges provide the minority of relatively
adequately trained teachers in the public primary schools and

lower-stream secondary schools. The university provides those Jamaicans who teach in the academic secondary schools. The large, popular sector has a majority of unqualified teachers, poor attendances, lack of facilities and overcrowded classrooms. The élite sector has luxurious staff-student ratios, comparatively well-trained teachers, high attendances and good facilities.

Mobility between these two sub-systems is low. Entry to academic secondary schools is regulated largely by examinations, and although candidates from public primary schools are supposed to take 70 per cent of the places on a reserved basis, students from these schools are at a great disadvantage. In 1970, 22,495 children sat the Common Entrance Examination for entry to secondary (grammar) schools, 85 per cent of them from public primary schools. There were 2,030 free places awarded, and just the official minimum of 70 per cent went to children from public primary schools. However, there is a certain amount of evasion of the regulations—children attend private schools, and join government schools in the final terms, just before the examination, in order to qualify for quota places. Moreover, the urban schools attended by the children of skilled workers and salaried people were very successful; the poorer urban schools were less successful; and the rural schools were very unsuccessful indeed.

Dr Douglas Manley made a study of the relative success of various schools and social groups in the examination, soon after the introduction of the system. The urban high schools were most successful, followed by the rural high schools. In the junior sector, urban private schools provided 7 per cent of the entry but took 13 per cent of all free places between 1957 and 1961. Rural private schools provided 2·4 per cent of the entry and took 3·7 per cent of free places. Urban primary schools as a group did not do badly—with 13 per cent of the entry they won nearly 22 per cent of the free places. However, rural primary schools, with 68 per cent of the entry, won only 33 per cent of the free places.[4]

These figures do not fully reflect the inequalities, however, since urban public schools cater for different social classes in different areas, and a few are known to be very successful, while others hardly ever win free places. (The successful schools are well known, and in Kingston they are described as having 'been taken over by the middle-class'.) It is more revealing to examine performance in the entrance examination in relation to parents' social class, as shown in Table 7.

TABLE 7   *Social class and success in common entrance examination*[5]

(a) *Social differences in size of entry and success in examination*

Group	Percentage of Entry	Free places
1 Professional, managerial	5·1	20·5
2 Teachers	4·9	7·3
3 Clerical	21·8	36·3
4 Skilled and semi-skilled	29·4	24·3
5 Unskilled workers	12·5	4·7
6 Farmers	26·3	6·8

(b) *Percentage of entry from each social class which won free places*[5]

Group	Percentage
1 Élite	66·3
2 Professional and managerial	45·8
3 Teachers	16·4
4 Clerical	18·5
5 Skilled and semi-skilled	9·2
6 Unskilled workers	4·2
7 Farmers	2·8

Obviously, the better-off the parents of a child the more likely they are to pay for his secondary education even though he fails to win a scholarship. Thus the discrepancies are increased. The largest and most predictable differences are those between the highly-educated parents and the rest; but the differences between urban and rural areas are also very marked. The difference exists even between parish capitals and rural districts. Thus in a survey of the parish of Manchester, Dr Eyre found that 'A hypothetical "average child" in Mandeville (the parish capital) has a twenty times greater chance of going to a secondary school than his counterpart by the south coast.' Most rural districts in the parish sent under 3 per cent of the appropriate age-group to secondary schools.[6]

The technical high schools, comprehensive schools and vocational schools, which prepare children for skilled jobs, are much more open to candidates from public primary schools, but they are very small—in 1972, their total enrolment was less than 9,000. Thus they cannot begin to compensate for the failure of the primary schools to provide children of the poorer classes with a chance of winning a good secondary education.

These figures are unfortunately not all up-to-date, and recently all places at secondary schools have been made free—that is, virtually all are now awarded on the basis of the Common Entrance Examination, and paid for by government. This will reduce the gross discrepancies, but the overall pattern will probably be much the same.

This brief survey of the educational system suggests that while channels of social mobility are open, they are structured in such a way that parental social class remains the best guide by far to the prospects of a child. In particular, it reveals the deprived condition of children of unskilled workers and small farmers. Obviously, this is not an unusual state of affairs; similar studies reveal that preferential treatment in education is normally given to the privileged, in all societies. None the less the extreme polarities in Jamaica clearly reflect the gross social divisions and material advantages within the population, and these are acute. I would estimate that today the chances of a small-holder's child getting into an academic secondary school and so perhaps entering a clerical or even professional career are perhaps 3 in 100. This would rise to 7 in 100 for the child of an urban worker, and to virtually 100 per cent for the children of the upper-middle-class.

Ironically, the educational system, which so obviously maintains the existing structure of privilege, is a crucial ideological support of the social system. In the first place, the system is believed by and large to reward merit; and since education is the major prerequisite for high occupational positions, these again can be justified as having been won, by meritorious performance, in an open competition. The fact is that 'education' is normally the consequence, not the cause, of high social position; but this is not generally recognized. The hopes pinned by the deprived on 'education' for their children are pathetic and unrealistic, but they are a vital support for the present structure of the society.[7]

A further ideological dimension may be discerned. Traditionally

74

in Jamaica 'race' was believed to determine the ability to assume power or to occupy high positions in government and business. Today there is a strong counter-belief that all men are potentially able to take responsibility and enjoy high status, but that the key requirement is 'education', which is achieved. The failure of the poor, largely black population in the slums and countryside to succeed through educational channels not only gives some reinforcement to traditional racialist attitudes, but, even more, it provides a new and independent justification for their deprived situation. They are 'foolish', 'rude', 'ignorant', and 'illiterate', and therefore are quite rightly unsuccessful in the pursuit of wealth, status and influence.[8] These oppositions tie up, perhaps, with the old 'Africa–England' opposition—culture today is acquired, in schools, and rewarded by skilled and highly-paid work; its lack is due to educational failure. 'Education' is thus a functional alternative to 'race' in the ideological justification of Jamaican social inequality, but it is much better adapted to contemporary conditions. It presents itself as open to achievement, and as a channel for social mobility.

Part three

Village and Slum

Chapter 12

A Village in the Hills

I have been concerned with processes operating at the level of Jamaican society as a whole, and perhaps at this stage a shift in perspective would be helpful. I shall describe two localities; first a rural area in the centre of the island, 'in the hills', where I spent six months on coming to Jamaica, and where I began to recognize the underlying principles of social relations on the island. I shall then briefly discuss the Kingston area, and in particular a slum in which I carried out a field-study over a four-month period. No community is 'typical' in every way, and, of course, a Kingston slum is a very special social environment. None the less, every Jamaican experiences his society to some extent through the particular prism of his immediate face-to-face contacts, and so a move from the general level of analysis helps to bring the situation of the individual into focus. Moreover, Jamaica is a single society, complex and differentiated, yet shot through with overriding social processes and accepted principles; and every local social arena exhibits these, and their effects, in a concrete and specific fashion. [1]

The village in which I settled with my family lay a few miles west of Christiana, the market town which has grown rich on the local speciality, the 'Irish potato'. The Christiana area is well-off by Jamaican country standards, and in addition to potatoes it produces a rich harvest of yams, table vegetables and, here and there, bananas. [2]

The village is loosely defined in practice as the region served by the village post office. It is a general service-centre, with shops, church, school, and even a small library. The village of D . . . was once a market-centre too, but it lost its market, and its police station, to Christiana, over fifty years ago.

Local people talk of the area, including the village, as being divided up into various 'districts', demarcated by the boundaries of the old estates. Within these 'districts' one finds several clusters of homesteads, each with an unofficial nickname.

Taking a broader view, one can see how the large estates, now as ever, provide the framework for the social geography of the area. Today a number of the large estates have been sold to bauxite companies, though some have been leased back to the original owners at a nominal rental. At the edges of the large estates are the crowded pockets of smallholders and landless labourers. The village itself, the third form of settlement, is, physically, a straggle of shops, churches, businesses and homes, which follow the main road for perhaps a mile. Some of the people living here are smallholders, whose holding simply happened to back onto the road when it was laid. However, it is here that one finds the local 'middle-class' too, the teachers, ministers, shop-keepers, commuters, and a few of the larger farmers who work mainly rented land. Many of these people are not natives of the area. Villages were often started by a grant of land from a land-owner who wanted a local market, and other services, but they are today independent social worlds.

The very lay-out of the area draws attention to the three main categories of local people—the large landowners in their isolated 'great houses' or, less grandly, in modern suburban homes; the smallholders and other labourers, in densely-crowded cottages; and the middle-class of the village. Further acquaintance im-mediately suggests reservations. Some of the teachers and shop-keepers do some farming, and some of the large farmers are intermarried with the village middle-class. Moreover, the small farmers are themselves divided into strata, and do not always see themselves as forming a single group *vis-à-vis* the large farmers or the other villagers.

Certainly in terms of economic function the division is useful. The large farmers are employers, or lease out land; the small farmers tend to rely upon them for occasional work, for land to rent, or for other favours. The middle-class serves as brokers between the local, farming community and the national economy and culture and services, though the tradesmen in the market town and the officials there are more powerful. The farmers are local, but many of the middle-class people are 'spiralists', moving up national professional hierarchies by way of successive postings in different parts of the island.

Other social processes tend to intensify or modify these class divisions. Some of the large farmers, the 'gentry', do not form close links with local people, and tend even to distance themselves to varying degrees from many 'Jamaican' values, preferring to stress 'English' values. They are linked by kinship and marriage with upper-class families in other parishes, and often also in England and Canada. Most of the large farmers, however, do not aspire to high national status on the old-fashioned scale. They intermarry locally, with one another and with the leading commercial people in the market town, are friendly with poorer people, and provide the political leadership of the constituency. To a certain extent, the distinction between these two groups is coded by colour values; certainly the 'gentry' are white, or, as they say, 'Jamaican white'. Other 'white' large farmers, however, usually of more humble origin, have taken coloured wives, and some coloured farmers in other parts of the island are of clear 'gentry' status.

The service middle-class can be divided into the skilled *v.* the shop-keepers; the former, school teachers, ministers and commuters, being generally outsiders, while the shop-keepers are usually local people, or at any rate settle for life in the village. Small shop-keepers and tradesmen (tailors, cobblers, mechanics, etc.) are often virtually indistinguishable from the small farmers in most ways, while a few large shop-keepers may be the equals of the large farmers and local semi-professionals, with whom they form friendship networks. In this area a further distinction isolated the skilled, mobile population, from the other people in the village. They were generally supporters of the Peoples' National Party (PNP), while the D . . . area was solidly behind the Jamaica Labour Party (JLP), at least at this time.

The small farmers also range in status, and one can identify various ideal types along the range. At the bottom is the landless labourer, often without much hope of improvement; in the middle, the man with three or four acres, renting a couple of acres from absent neighbours or large landlords, and occasionally working as a labourer; and at the top, a handful of men who control considerable acreages, mainly of rented land, or land they manage for a landlord. Such people might have a considerable income, employ a number of labourers, and sub-let some land to neighbours. Their life-style sometimes approaches that of the large farmer, but they always show deference to the established large farmers. It is from their ranks that the unofficial 'mayors' of the districts come, the so-called village lawyers, Papa This or That, enjoying considerable influence in local affairs.[3]

Mobility for a smallholder's child into a higher social class is usually a consequence of migration, or rather education plus migration. I found no example of a man beginning without considerable capital and yet becoming a large landowner. The 'kulaks' were rather men who through luck or skilful management of personal relationships with rich and powerful landholders managed to acquire managerial control over, or the right to rent, significant areas of farmland.

The social horizons of each of these categories of the population varied. The 'gentry' saw themselves sometimes as members of a grand imperial class; the large farmers as members of the parish establishment; the skilled middle-class, as part of a national category; the shop-keepers, as part of a commercial network centred on the market town. The smallholders had the most restricted social universe; their lives, their marriages, their relationships were concentrated within a few miles of the place of their birth—with one crucial exception. Virtually everyone in the village, except perhaps the poorest, had relatives not only in Kingston but brothers, sisters, children, or even parents in Britain and North America. Thus while they are the most rooted and the most parochial of the social strata, they too are familiar with other worlds, as real possibilities for themselves.

A general characteristic of social judgments was the emphasis placed on reputation or 'respect'. This is particularly strong among the local, poorer people, for whom it implies (among other things) the possession of a tidy and comfortable house, marriage, regular attendance at a recognized church, 'decent' dress, and the avoidance of 'cussing bad word', gambling and public drunkennness. A poor man who achieves some sort of financial coup will adjust his behaviour immediately—a friend of mine was a local scapegrace until the death of his father suddenly landed him with the control of perhaps a hundred acres of cultivation, when he quickly moved in with his stepmother, stopped frequenting the bars, and even began to contemplate marriage to the woman with whom he had been living for several years. Economic status, however, remains the crucial determinant of social prestige; the display of 'respect' can only modify this basic status within fairly narrow limits. At the top of the social scale, members of the rural upper-classes are evaluated by the general population mainly on the basis of their 'kindness' and political affiliation. They are popular or unpopular, but virtually nothing they do can shake their solid status.

Colour corresponds loosely to social status. At the bottom, in this area at least, the poor people were all black. Members of the local middle-class were generally black, but included some coloured people, and the occasional white wife. At the higher levels one found all the local whites—except for a drunk and broken former businessman who had retired, in old age, to the village, and lived in some isolation, on the earnings of his coloured wife. However, members of the rural upper-middle class varied in colour from 'white' to 'black' (including a black spinster in the market town, who had been a Senator and owned a chemist's shop). At a party within this stratum one might come across the whole gamut of Jamaican racial types, and even within a family party the range of colour was often striking—and little remarked, explicitly or implicitly. Even in the immediate area there were several examples of 'intermarriage'—between dark Jamaican men and foreign white, or light Jamaican women, and between 'white' farmers and educated coloured women. Such marriages were not the subject of particular comment, though they may have been at first. Some members of the 'white' older generation had more exclusive notions about colour, but even in a homogeneous circle their judgments tended to stress a broader notion of status, embracing wealth, education, respectability and colour—colour sometimes providing the idiom of judgment (often implicitly) but not the determinant.

It was here, in the country, where attitudes are probably more conservative, that I first became aware of the situational varia-ability of the identification of 'colour' values. For example, I was present on occasions when both a wealthy 'brown' stock-farmer and a poor Chinese-Negro taxi-driver, talking in a rum-shop to a black audience, emphatically insisted upon identifying themselves with the audience, in colour terms. They talked of 'we of the naygur race', and the taxi-driver even asserted the identity of Chinese and Africans in racial terms. On the other hand, I was once walking along the village street when I came across a brown Cayman lady talking to the 'white' lady who lived in the local great house. She went on, at some length, to both of us about the way in which 'they' are now hostile to 'we' light-skinned folk. In both situations the audience was slightly resistant to the classification employed, but did not reject it. In each case the speaker assumed the existence, and acceptance of clearly-defined and significant colour categories, but the speaker's own anomalous status implicitly contradicted this central contention, at least to the extent that the audience allowed the speaker to classify himself or herself with them. The pitfalls of dogmatizing about folk colour-consciousness were quickly apparent.

Collecting genealogies and family histories, other significant assumptions emerged. Apparently 'black' people would claim 'white' (often, for some reason, Scots) ancestors, while perhaps not being able to locate the relevant ancestor with any certainty on a genealogy. Not always, however—one man told me a long and confused anecdote about his dying white grandmother being brought out of her hut on a stretcher to view her grandson. Informants also sometimes stressed the black ancestry in distinguished and apparently 'white' local families. The general principle, that all Jamaicans are of mixed racial ancestry, would often be stated straightforwardly, by members of all strata, sometimes with an element of either defiance or shame, since they could not be sure how such revelations would strike me. People from England, it was generally assumed, usually correctly, would be more touchy about racial purity than were Jamaicans.

The other principle, that 'white' was higher in status than 'black', was also widely accepted, and poor informants would talk of families having gone 'up' or 'down' over the generations as a consequence of successive marriages with lighter and darker people. People sometimes spoke of themselves as simply black, but more commonly as being lighter or darker than others, and others were often identified, or described partly with reference to their 'complexion'. However, anomalies were so readily accepted, and the colour value generally so secondary, that status was never assumed to be directly related to colour except at the top and bottom of the ladder: the very rich were expected to be white, the very poor, black. The relationship between poverty and blackness was best expressed by an informant of Madeline Kerr, but he spoke in terms the people of D . . . might have used—[4]

> The people here honour the higher colour more than the black. If I went to my bed and woke in the morning as a white man I would be in an entirely different position though still poor. If I were white and worked in rags and bare-footed, as I often do, it would make a lot of difference that I am white. The people in lower social class would respect me and the people in higher class would try to raise me up to themselves and to the level that I ought to be as a white man. It is easier for the poor white man to come up in life than for the poor black man. The higher classes of people do not recognize the poor black man. They recognize anyone who is in a high financial standing.

Here, succinctly stated, is the whole nexus of status—mode of work, clothes, 'respect', money and colour. In a sense that most rural people would agree upon, the passage would be equally valid if for 'white' the speaker had substituted well-dressed, in clerical employment, or even speaking standard English. The giveaway is in the last two sentences: colour is a symbol, rather than a determinant, of status; and not the central symbol.

Education was respected by everyone, although the upper-class farmers rarely had more than some secondary schooling. Older members of the élite sometimes fell short even of this level, particularly the women, but their children were all sent to private preparatory and grammar schools. Members of the lower class were usually only just literate, if at all, and their aspirations for their children did not realistically go further than the technical high school, a standard few achieved despite the fact that one of the few technical high schools in the island was in the immediate vicinity. The marginal members of the middle-class, particularly primary school teachers, used their position to gain access to grammar schools. They would send their children to private preparatory schools in Christiana, and then withdraw them and place them in the primary school of the village shortly before the grammar school entrance examination. This did not imply loss of status for them, and it enabled their children to compete for scholarship places within the broader allocation made for candidates from government primary schools. Most of the successful candidates from the local primary schools were of this type; indeed, few others were even prepared for the examinations. The schools worked on the principle that their highest goal was the technical secondary school, and their normal fate early termination of education.

Caribbean sociology has always stressed the different institutional forms characterizing lower and higher classes, and in particular the differences in family form and religious expression. In the D . . . area, I found, the big farmers and members of the middle-class tend to have stable marriages, and to pursue the fortunes of their children by means of education and sponsored migration. The poorer people have a remarkably similar set of aspirations, though they are less commonly successful in achieving them. Most of the men, of all classes, enjoyed pre-marital and extra-marital liaisons, but upper-class men did not openly live with their mistresses.

The majority of adults in the community are partners in stable conjugal unions, but the higher one moved up the scale the more frequently had these been solemnized in church. The tendency among respectable smallholders was to marry fairly late, often after many years of conjugal life. However, many poor people in the area had been married in church, as a consequence of the energetic insistence of the wife of a Moravian missionary. This did not seem to make any difference to anyone, except, presumably the missionary's wife, and she had departed several years before my visit. Common-law wives take their husband's name and enjoy in practice the same rights as church wives; nor are their children regarded as stigmatized, although 'outside' children, the children of a woman who is not living in a conjugal union, do suffer some discrimination, particularly from their fathers' families, and half-siblings.

In all these households the majority of the children have no choice but to leave the area on adolescence or early adulthood. Men never divide their land, and therefore their sons are denied profitable employment at home. One son may remain at home, doing odd jobs, on the understanding that he will inherit the right to farm his father's land; and a daughter may help her mother as an itinerant petty-trader ('higgler'), or as a washerwoman. For the rest, legitimate and illegitimate alike, there is no option.

These considerations apply in almost equal strength to large farmers. The maintenance of an appropriate style is impossible for more than one or perhaps two sons, but the family is likely to have the necessary connections to find business openings for other children, even if they have not been very successful at school. Members of this class seem often to emigrate to Canada, now in any case the new Jamaican Eldorado.

The genealogies of smallholders rarely go back further than two generations, and (perhaps surprisingly) there is little tendency to favour the mother's side. The shallow depth of genealogies is accompanied by a narrow geographical spread of relatives, for most marriages are made within a radius of less than two or three miles. In consequence, most local people have a host of kin among their neighbours; indeed, middle-class people will say, 'You can't say anything about anyone in D . . ., they're all related.' At the same time, few can trace precise links, and are content to say, e.g., 'My mother called her niece, so I call her cousin.'

A number of large farmers, particularly the lighter coloured, can trace their genealogies in the male line to their last European-born ancestor. The spread of kin in this group varies with the distinction I drew between the 'gentry' and other large farmers. The gentry have most of their kin and affines in other districts, or abroad, while the other large farmers have many ties (particularly through marriage) with large farmers in the region of the market town, or with traders there.

The mother–child bond is very strong, as are ties between children of one mother. However, marital ties also tend, in all classes, to generate economic assistance. Smallholders linked by marriage co-operate in farming operations, while the large farmers combine in economic ventures with affines, particularly affines in business in the market town.

If there is a unity beneath the class variations in family organization, the same is true in the field of religion. There is a strong association of the 'established' churches with solid class standing, while the more ecstatic religion of the balm-yard churches attracts a poorer and less respectable congregation. But the pattern is not rigid, except, once again, at the top and bottom of the scale. The respectable citizens of D . . . attend the Baptist Missionary Church, the Anglican Church, or a nearby Moravian Church.

The poorer people are divided between these, the Church of God (a half-way house, in both secular and theological terms), and the two less orthodox churches, with their priestesses and more expressive rituals. There is, then, a gradation in the social standing of the churches, and this is matched by their ritual style; but no one church is unequivocally the church of the gentry or large farmers, or of the middle-class; and the mass of the people (except the poorest, who cannot afford a Sunday suit) may attend any church.

None the less, the doctrinal unity of all the churches in the area is striking; they are all fundamentalist Protestant churches, which rely on inspiration, conversion, and song. They are not only fundamentalist: they are all apocalyptic. Death is near, the end of the world is at hand. The blessed will be saved, the wicked damned. Salvation has outer signs—dress, behaviour, 'respect'. Overt biblical references are particularly favoured by the poor, but these basic ideas are shared by the members of all classes, to whom the Bible is a constant source of reference and interest.

The churches and the schools, ideologically the most powerful institutions in the area, both predicate the division of humanity into two camps, but each operates in terms of a moral and in general unseen dichotomy. The churches talk of the saved and the damned, the good and the bad. Dress neatly, mind your language and remember God. The end is nigh. The schools support this enthusiastically,[5] but add that the dichotomy is also between the educated and deferential, and the ignorant and unruly. The division of the society by wealth, style and colour, the oppositions which depend upon outward signs, are ignored or reinterpreted. Consequently these ideological statements inhibit any tendency of the system towards class-opposition, exacerbated by colour identification. They also implicitly justify the differences in wealth and status in the country, not by appealing to a kingdom of God where injustices will be righted, as in quietist faiths, but by suggesting that people succeed because they live in ways which are pleasing to God, and because they are educated. The wealthy and successful can therefore dismiss the poor as failures, Godless, illiterate and idle, who through bad behaviour have forfeited their chances both in this world and in the next.

There is another institutional force which pulls against class formation, and that is the organization of the political parties.

The D . . . area was a JLP stronghold, but some neighbouring areas were equally strongly for the PNP. That was the general pattern in country areas: a patchwork of divisions, each over-whelmingly for one particular party. In the 1972 General Election, voters in polling stations in the village favoured the JLP by over three to one, while the proportions were reversed in two neigh-bouring areas.[6] The only open supporters of the PNP in the village were a few teachers, commuters, a large shopkeeper (who complained that she was being boycotted in consequence), and a stubborn old peasant, rich and illiterate, who complained that the JLP-controlled Land Authority had refused to build a road to his house. Thus local people were united politically, or at least the mass of the people were united with the large farmers, and together they shared a strong and emotional political identification, and an opposition to neighbouring communities, and to some members of the transient middle-class.

On a broader level, the middle-class and upper-class villagers associated with political comrades at the constituency level, and in some cases participated in party organization. They formed two blocs in the constituency, and friendships between people of different political persuasion were rare.

Political victory was regarded as an opportunity for the just rewarding of the faithful, and the most was made of opportunities for patronage, by parish councillors and members of parliament. In addition, there was in the area the first of Jamaica's Land Authorities. Its governing committee was appointed by the governing party in the country, and was always made up entirely of members of that party. Controlling grants and jobs as well as other favours, it was a powerful machine, and it was used cynically. The main beneficiaries of victory are the better-off supporters of the winning party, since it is they who become members of the Land Authority, co-operative committees, etc. This does not necessarily involve direct corruption, and many people enjoy office for its own sake, but there have also been fortunes made by those properly placed even on local bodies. However, every party supporter believed that he would benefit in a direct fashion from his loyalty if his party won: best of all, if it won both locally and nationally.

Although the expectation of concrete material favours is central to local political affairs, it is not sufficient to explain the emotional commitment of the people to their parties, or their interest in broadly ideological questions and in the personalities of the leaders. Identification with the leader and the party links members of different classes in the area, in one organization and in a shared desire for a largely impersonal triumph. Political loyalty is an aspect of community loyalty; who one is, politically speaking, is defined by being a person of D . . ., not by being poor or rich, black or white. The large shop-keeper who was a PNP activist had come to the village fifteen odd years before. His wife, a light-coloured woman, was the cousin of the MP, a former JLP minister, and a white man. She urged the black PNP candidate to go into a poor district near the village and encourage the people to 'vote their race'. But they remained loyal to her white cousin, and regarded her as an outsider, not because of her colour or material success, but because of her politics.

Chapter 13

Kingston and its Slums

The only general study of Kingston is by a geographer, Dr. C. G. Clarke,[1] but there have been various surveys of particular aspects of urban living, mainly by government agencies, and dealing with housing, household budgets, etc. In the slum areas a number of studies have been made of the religious cults which have flourished for many years, and in particular of the Rastafarian movement which grew up in the last generation. These studies have generally concentrated upon the idiom and ideology of the movement, and rather neglected its social basis. During my stay in the capital I did some fieldwork with a small gang of young men in Majesty Pen, one of the poorest of the government estates (where rents were 60 cents a week for a room). I also accompanied members of various social work agencies on case rounds.

Clarke has described the main ecological areas in the Corporate Area—the respectable north, the business area (now supplemented by the development at New Kingston in the centre), and the poorer areas in the West and East. Here he described the high-density tenement settlements and slum yards, which he distinguished from the poorest government housing areas, like that at Tower Hill, which, while of lower density, had a higher rate of unemployment, and finally the squatters' camps, on the fringe of the tenements and on the outskirts of the built-up area.

Clarke demonstrated the continuity of the ecological structure of the city. As in 1943, so in 1960[2]

the tenements, parts of East Kingston, and almost all West Kingston were low ranking, while areas of higher status were located to the north and east, and especially around Half Way Tree. This patterning of social statuses could be traced back to the 1870's, when King's House was established to the north of Half Way Tree, or, further, to the late eighteenth century, when Kingston's merchants had begun to purchase residential property on the Liguanea Plain. Furthermore, on the microscale, overcrowding and disease in West Kingston were reminiscent of conditions in some of the same parts of the city in 1850, while the squatter camps resembled the Negro huts of the period of slavery. Despite the high degree of continuity in the spatial arrangement of social statuses since slavery, certain recent changes were noteworthy. Parts of Central and East Kingston declined in status between 1943 and 1960 as their new inhabitants moved out to the suburbs. This was accompanied by a considerable expansion of the high status areas in central and northern St. Andrew. As a consequence, social polarisation and segregation were even more marked in 1960 than they had been in 1943. A major contributor to increasing polarisation in the city was the growth of the population and its concentration in West Kingston.

Inspection of maps revealed

a cartographic correlation between male household headship, marriage, denominational Christianity and secondary school education, modally concentrated in northern St. Andrew on the one hand, and consensual cohabitation or extra-residential mating, Afro-Christian cults and sects, and non-secondary education, concentrated in West Kingston on the other.

Moreover, 'the closer the cultural pattern conformed to the West European "norm", the higher the socio-economic status of the area'.[3] Educational level provided the best single clue to general socio-economic level, and 'socio-economic status was determined more by education than by race'.[4] None the less, 'Europeans' never lived in predominantly 'African' areas, and were concentrated overwhelmingly in élite suburbs. 'Africans' lived there too, but predominated in the poor areas.

Clarke was able to identify what he called Kingston's 'slums of despair', areas of the city in which people lived by 'scuffling' and 'cotching', without much hope of ever finding a job. These areas corresponded to the poorest government settlements, which had been built precisely for the poorest of the settlers in tenements and yards; and also, particularly, in the squatters' camps. Squatters represented perhaps 5 per cent of the city's population, and, like the people in the poor government settlements, they were largely urban-born. The rural immigrants tended to find places to live in the tenements and yards, and only a minority of the long-term casualties sank to the dubious haven of the 'slums of despair'. Here was the home of Rastafarian belief, and of a whole sub-culture:[5]

> The essence of 'cotching' and 'scuffling' was summarized
> by the phrase 'living on the dungle' (i.e., the rubbish-dump).
> During the 1930's people had literally done so, and even
> in 1960 one major squatter camp was situated on the
> seaward edge of the dump in West Kingston. Furthermore,
> as all the squatter settlements lay within easy reach of the
> dungle, it continued to act as a major source of saleable
> goods and building materials, and of food discarded by
> groceries, supermarkets, restaurants, and private households.
> Droves of squatters awaited the arrival of the garbage carts,
> and, as they disgorged their contents, competed with the
> buzzards for them. In this way the participants of the
> subculture maintained a parasitic relationship with the more
> prosperous inhabitants of the city.

My fieldwork was concentrated in such 'slums of despair', a poor government development, Majesty Pen, and its neighbour, the squatters' camp, Moonlight City. Both were settled largely by native Kingstonians, mainly engaged in home-crafts, fishing and scuffling, and either scorning or failing to find employment in 'Babylon', the modern industrial city. These were the areas I tentatively identified earlier, the seats of hard-core unemployment. They contrast strongly with tenement areas—a quarter of a mile down the Spanish Town road, driving into Kingston, one came to a tenement area where social workers reported that over 90 per cent of their clients were immigrants from rural areas, often dreadfully poor and suffering from social dislocations of great severity, but still in aspiration part of the mainstream of urban life. Better-off Kingstonians shunned the tenement areas and slums alike, but it was only in these very specific areas of native Kingstonian 'scuffler' communities that the rejection was whole-heartedly reciprocated, most explicitly in some versions of Rastafarian ideology.

Several points must be made to counter the negative impression of life in these communities which may have been conveyed. First of all, a number of useful, pleasant and reasonably profitable trades were plied by people in these areas—there were successful fishermen, carpenters, blacksmiths, potters, and traders in ganja (marijuana); and women were washerwomen, higglers and occasionally bar-girls and prostitutes. The characteristic shared by all these occupations was that they were outside the sphere of industrial organization (and domestic service); they were on the margins of the economy. People occupied in these ways could make a living, but they were not drawn into relationships of subordination in modern or traditional organizations.

Second, although the middle-class conceives of these areas as centres of crime, and they are liable to constant police interference and brutality, there are very few internal crimes. Gangs from a slum commit crimes elsewhere. In Majesty Pen people would leave boats and engines untended overnight, and shop-keepers took only casual security precautions. Intra-community violence was rare. Thus although removed from institutionalized control through employment, and alienated by popular attitudes and police violence, these communities were internally disciplined.

Third, despite the ideology of rejection and retreat, Rasta-farianism, which is particularly popular among younger men, for whom it is an idiom for the assertion of defiance and independence *vis-à-vis* the society at large, the values of the broader society are to a surprising degree accepted and acted upon. The decor of the homes strives towards bourgeois refinement, schools are strongly supported for the children, and friendly—egalitarian —ties with the occasional outsider are cherished.

Something of the tension between the assertion of distinction and the basic acceptance of the culture may be glimpsed in all sorts of situations—the tension is greatest among young men. For example, I participated in a conversation while visiting (with a Rastafarian friend) a ganja-den behind Coronation Market. (Ganja—marijuana—incidentally is a Jamaican working-class equivalent to beer in England or wine in some European countries. A distinguished psychiatrist has called it the 'benevolent alternative'.)[6]

The owner of the den told me the story of his life. He had nine children, and six were at school, one attending a leading grammar school at his own expense. The money came from a small grocery store which he ran, but he was a lessee, and his landlord suddenly evicted him. The boy had to leave school, and now everything was going wrong. There was no rice, no milk, no Government assistance. 'My hope is only from Ras Tafari' (Haile Selassie, the messiah of the Rastafarians). The others in the den joined in the lamentations at the state of the country, and quickly moved on to the state of the world. One young man said the 'youth' would rise. Another preferred the view that the Third World War, imminent in the Middle East, would bring the present system to an end. One old man, rejoining us and courteously complimenting the host on the state of his toilet, was particularly gloomy about the decline in the value of the American dollar.

Talk then turned to armed violence in Kingston, an issue greatly stressed by the mass media at the time. One man said one couldn't put a gun in the hands of an illiterate man. It was dangerous. Another man asked rhetorically whether an illiterate man could build a building.

It was agreed that the underlying problem was the decline in religion. 'We need just one leader, Christ God Almighty. And Haile Selassie is now Christ on earth, and we must all accept it. Ham, Shem and Japheth, Black, Brown and White; only Christ and Haile Selassie can unite them.'

The themes of this conversation were typical, and underlying the Rastafarian idiom employed by some of the participants was a fundamental acceptance of various values of the broader society, including the high valuation of religion, literacy and the power of reasoning, and a condemnation of violent crime and, at one level, of racialism. The messianic assumptions, and the wild notions of international affairs, were by no means peculiar to those influenced by the Rastafarian creed. Even university-educated professionals would seriously debate the coming apocalypse, the inevitable world war predicted in Revelations, and the international decline of morality.

Rastafarian ideology deserves specific consideration, nevertheless, since it represents in part an attempt by the Kingston poor to redefine their identity, and their destiny. Rastafarianism has roots in the long Jamaican folk tradition of religious messianism, in which Bedward and Garvey stand as direct precursors. Garvey is by far the greater influence, although much of his programme was developed in response to the plight of black America, and reflects American Negro traditions. In 1920 he began to concentrate on a huge movement to repatriate black ex-slaves to Africa, and in his teachings and writings he appealed to racial pride and loyalty. Despite the failure of his brief political career in Jamaica in the late 1920s, and the greater failure of his projected Black Star line, Garvey is the most revered of all Jamaicans for the Rastafarians, and for many others. His life is described in mythical terms, and many predict his return. He is also one of the official 'National Heroes', who are celebrated on the annual National Heroes' Day.[7]

The other main source of the Rastafarian movement is the medley of so-called pocomania churches, from which it grew directly in West Kingston after the Second World War.[8] Like those churches, it is diffusely organized in a series of communities and cult-groups, with rapidly-changing influence and membership. The present government has even encouraged the establishment of a branch of the Ethiopian Coptic Church, which has become part of the series of more or less 'Rastafarian' organizations. Individual leaders are very important, but their support is never secure. The movement is thus without a single leader or accepted central organization, and is diffuse and protean in form. Moreover, many identify themselves as Rastafarians only in some contexts, or as sympathizers with certain beliefs. The 'locksmen', who cultivate a distinctive 'African' appearance and style are a small, usually young, minority. Estimates of membership vary widely, but they are a strong force in the poorer slum areas, particularly in Government housing areas like Majesty Pen, and squatters' camps like Moonlight City, where Rastafarian emblems and decorations are everywhere, and 'locksmen' most commonly found.

Dr Barrett has provided a summary of the main tenets to which people calling themselves Rastafarians would generally subscribe:
1 Haile Selassie is the living god.
2 The black man is the reincarnation of ancient Israelites who

at the hand of the white man have been in exile in Jamaica.

3 The white man is inferior to the black man.

4 The Jamaican situation is a hopeless hell, Ethiopia is heaven.

5 The invincible Emperor of Ethiopia is now arranging for expatriated persons of African origin to return to Ethiopia.

6 In the near future the black man shall rule the world.[9]

The movement became prominent in the 1950s, and was a source of considerable anxiety to the Jamaican establishment, who particularly resented the Rastafarian claim that they were not Jamaicans (but rather Africans), and who were disturbed by the symbolism and forms of expression used by the Rastafarians, and often deliberately used to shock—the hair-style of the locksmen, based on photographs of Masai warriors; the common use of 'rude' language and abrupt challenges; the heavy use of ganja, generally associated at that time with criminal violence. However, in the 1960s the movement achieved a certain respectability, and Rastafarian arts and crafts, and in particular their music, enjoyed a growing vogue. There were various reasons for this—the sympathetic university report of 1960,[10] which influenced government policy despite the initially hostile reaction of many elements of the establishment; the increasing recognition that they did not constitute a political threat; and the general diffusion of Black Power theory. Today the educated Jamaican, and a strong element of the established 'middle-class' concede to the Rastafarians an authenticity of style which, while reflecting a patronizing and distant regard, is a measure of their incorporation into the wider society.[11] When in 1973 an upper-middle-class light lady of conservative opinions held a 'Rasta' party, at which guests had to wear some Rastafarian gear, this was not only a satirical gesture against what she regarded as a ludicrous new acceptance of the Rastafarians; it was also a recognition that they had arrived.

The ideology is obviously one of retreat or rejection from Jamaican society and values, if in many central respects it simply inverts them—Africa replaces England, black replaces white, at the top of the classic totem-pole. However, it is not to be read too literally. Masses of Jamaicans, including some of the poorest, actually did migrate, in a somewhat messianic spirit, to Britain. Hardly any have gone to Africa, and few seriously plan to—Africa, for them, is also somewhat like the Israel of medieval Jewry, a paradise which will come into its own with the messianic age. Similarly, there is some tendency to deny the racialism which seems to be at the core of the movement. When Professor M. G. Smith made the first study of the Rastafarians, fifteen years ago, one of the most radical leaders became a friend. They met again recently at a boxing championship at the National Stadium, and the Rastafarian said to him enthusiastically, 'You see, I predicted this to you fifteen years ago: black and white sitting together as one.' In politics, too, a number of Rastafarians support the present prime minister, Michael Manley, perhaps because of his deliberate adoption of some Rastafarian symbols during the election.

What remains central is the mystical and cultural content of the movement. The Rastafarians have affected the meaning of 'Africa' for the mass of Jamaicans. At the heart of their dogma is the assertion of the supremacy of black values, and the symbolic reversal of the value system of Jamaica, which they often enjoy referring to as 'Babylon'. The prediction which Smith and his colleagues made in 1960 that the movement was liable to imminent politicization based on the identification of black and proletariat has not been fulfilled despite the efforts of the occasional radical intellectual to help it on its way.

The 'slums of despair' are the symbols of the threatening masses for those who identify themselves as 'middle-class'.[12] They are also the source of some fashionable youth styles, and the hope of revolution for some romantic intellectuals. Their Rastafarian intelligentsia take their role very seriously, as well they might. They are regularly starred in films and television programmes, and a minor Rastafarian leader will tell one how the Ambassador of X visited him last year, to take the pulse of the working classes.

I have tried to put these slums in a more realistic perspective. This is necessary in order to demystify various fashionable (foreign and home-made) models of the social environment of Kingston. The 'slums of despair' are not the home of the most numerous, much less the most characteristic group of poor Kingstonians. They are important because they contain many people, particularly women and children, living in dreadful poverty; and also because they have come to stand for so much, both for Jamaicans and for others trying to understand Jamaica. They form one pole of a structure, the élite of St Andrew and foreign tourists providing the other, which is a potent source of rhetorical fever. Virtually all Jamaicans, except the inhabitants of these slums, blame them for the city's crimes, and they are subject to intermittent but bloody harassment from the police. 'Rastas' and 'rich whites' do not make up Jamaica, except for television crews. But they provide useful reference points for the self-definition, by contrast, of the 'ordinary Jamaican'.

Part four

Politics and Social Change

Chapter 14

Race and the Changing Jamaica
—Public and Private Contexts

Jamaica became independent in 1962, but universal suffrage was introduced in 1944, and the black masses had made a decisive entry into the political arena in 1938, and in the trade union movement which followed from the labour disturbances of that year. These political developments have had crucial implications for the meaning of race in contemporary Jamaica, but they have operated in the context of other relevant forces and movements. The developments in public life and the political environment that must be stressed in the analysis of modern Jamaica include the following:

1 The fact that people of African ancestry have come to dominate the political and administrative structures. As in all formerly colonial states, this helps to undermine the old sense of black impotence and dependence.

2 The related fact that political leaders are now ultimately dependent upon popular support, and that in consequence the black masses, recently politically marginal, now have a sense of their political importance.

3 These developments coincided with the highly-publicized emergence of the Rastafarian movement in Jamaica and of the various Black Power movements in the USA. All of these stemmed in part from the ideas of the Jamaican Marcus Garvey, who was officially declared a 'National Hero', though, like most prophets, he had enjoyed little honour at home in his lifetime.

4 Both Black Power and the Rastafarian movement were part of the international politicization of 'race', which was such a feature of the 1960s. This was related, in turn, to the political emergence of Black Africa, perhaps particularly Nkrumah's Ghana. The new international, political meaning of 'blackness' has been very important in Jamaica.

5 All these developments combined to draw attention to the continued metropolitan domination of the economy, and to one of the symbols of Jamaica's poverty and dependence, the tourists.

6 Finally, all this coincided with a period of massive Jamaican emigration, first to the United Kingdom and then to North America, a movement which also has relevance to the interpretation of racial symbols.

The most obvious impact of these developments has been to make 'race' an explicit, public, political concern in a way that it had not been for many years. The nationalist movement was dominated by the educated coloured and black Jamaicans, as are the political parties which derive from it. While anti-imperialist sentiment has always been muted in Jamaica, in comparison to many ex-colonies, the nationalist movement made it less attractive for even traditionally anglophile middle-class 'brown' people to continue to glorify British culture and institutions. The notion of 'one nation' has become the political orthodoxy, at least as an ideal. Moreover, the new political leaders have been obliged to compete for the support of large numbers of black, poor Jamaicans, and experiments have been made with various racial appeals.

Direct Black Power appeals have been tried without much success. What has been of greater significance is the attempt made by politicians to gain a reputation for being positively identified with the aspirations of the black poor. This has involved symbolic gestures in the direction of 'African' values, particularly as these have been positively redefined by the Rastafarians. The broad message is that the 'sufferer', the 'little man', etc. is the true Jamaican, who has first call on the attentions of the politicians and the resources of the country. As part of this message, politicians on the make lead symbolic attacks on the rich, white world—tourists are abused, dress conventions challenged, etc. In these ways, the politicians have reversed the accepted values in dramatic public statements and gestures, in order to suggest that they will reverse, or at least improve, the distribution of wealth and opportunity.

An example may illustrate these strategies. It is provided by the technique used in the 1972 general election by Michael Manley, then leader of the opposition and now Prime Minister. The slogan *Power for the People*, associated with a Black Power salute, carried with it an appeal to the notion that the real 'People'

were the black masses. The message was enriched by the promin-
ence given to Reggae protest songs with[1]

words that came straight from the Old Testament, largely
reflecting Rastafarian speech patterns and a 'sufferers'
philosophy. Thus the message, though couched in biblical
language, was obvious to all who shared common experiences.
'Beat down Babylon' said 'O what a wicked situation, I and
I dying from starvation'; *'Small Axe'* was saying that it
takes a small axe to chop a big tree; *'Must get a Beating'* ·
said, 'I can't stand this no longer, the wicked getting
stronger'.

These themes were developed further in the presentation of
Michael Manley as 'Joshua' (to his father's Moses), leading the
oppressed into the promised land. Joshua's rod, a walking stick
given to Manley by the Ethiopian Emperor (and the Rastafarian
messiah) came to have a major symbolic function.[2]

Thousands of Jamaicans came to believe that the Rod was
imbued with supernatural powers, and everywhere he
appeared people wanted to touch this potent source of
power, a few ascribing to it healing properties.
    Thus when Mr. Edward Seaga (JLP Kingston West)
claimed that he had 'found' Joshua's Rod, newspaper
readers may have chuckled but to the PNP it was no
laughing matter for he had struck at the very heart of the
mystique.
    The PNP took out a full page press advertisement to
assert that 'Seaga's stick is not Joshua's Rod', giving a minute
description of the 'true' Rod. The 'finding' of the Rod
coincided with Manley's return to Kingston from his rural
campaign, and a constituency rally provided the occasion
for a stage-managed demonstration that Joshua was still in
possession of the true Rod. According to newspaper accounts,
to shouts of 'The Rod, Joshua, The Rod' an orange wrapped
box was held aloft by the Prime Minister's mother, Mrs.
Edna Manley, and Miss Beverley Anderson (who later
became Mrs. Michael Manley). To high drama, the box
was opened and Mr. Manley dramatically held the Rod

aloft. 'Let us touch it, let us hold the power', the crowd shouted as they passed towards the platform seeking to touch the out-stretched rod. The PNP could breathe again, the legitimacy of the Rod had been re-established.

Manley was talking a language which embodied the beliefs of many poor Jamaicans, but using a modern idiom. This was not a traditional use of folk dialect and fundamentalist theology, though it did recall these sources, and even earlier messianic movements in Jamaica. Rather this was a modern, urban, even romantic idiom, immediately attractive to the young and representing at the same time a call as one of themselves to the ordinary poor Jamaican, and a suggestion of ferment and change. It depended upon the rehabilitation of 'African' symbols and other elements of the popular culture, but it was far from Millard Johnson's crude appeal to racial loyalties. It was also more than just a way of attracting popular support. Through political rituals of this kind the values of people are influenced, their self-image bolstered, and the legacy of past denigration is lightened. It is worth re-marking that such techniques have been most successfully employed by two light-coloured politicians, Manley himself and Edward Seaga of the opposition JLP; and also that both have married well-known black Jamaican beauties.

One cannot dismiss this sort of thing as merely symbolic or as cynical vote-mongering. The historical depreciation of blackness and African-ness in Jamaica was achieved by the manipulation of symbols, and these symbolic gestures help to liberate people from ingrained feelings of inadequacy and impotence. One effect of these dramas is to frighten some light-coloured Jamaicans, whose own self-esteem is tied up with traditional evaluations of colour and of cultural traditions, and who see these symbolic assaults as presaging an assault upon their privileges, and even their personal security. This again is not just fantasy. The new politicization of race, and related symbols, has led to an increase in overtly racial abuse directed by poor blacks towards well-to-do and light-coloured people in public places. Symbolic reversals of the traditional value-system have helped to undermine the whole traditional structure of deference. It is true that these things are merely symbolic as opposed to the continued inequalities in

Jamaica. But this does not mean that the politicians are being cynical. It would take a very cool man to disrupt these attitudes while deliberately calculating to maintain the established system of privilege.

Attempts have been made to win votes on a straightforward racial appeal, and these have failed. This reflects the fact that Jamaican society is not organized, even implicitly, into racial blocs. The real meaning of race in Jamaica is as one of the symbols of status, and as one aspect of the definition of identity. Politically, then, race and racial symbols refer to the kind of things for which one stands. This makes much more comprehensible the popularity of light-skinned élite politicians like Manley and Seaga. A similar lesson may be learnt from the tendency among Black Power intellectuals at the University to talk of being 'black' or 'white' as a function of one's beliefs rather than one's colour.[3] They have not convincingly related 'colour' and 'class' in Jamaica, but they recognize implicitly that the central issue is the recasting of the notion of the true Jamaican. The politicians symbolically affirm the legitimate claim of the 'real' Jamaican identity, and the demand that government should serve the mass of the population, not, as in the past, a small and privileged group.

It is in this context that the occasional scapegoating of tourists, and the formal intellectual rejection of them must be put. They represent the antithesis to the real Jamaican, and their activities have great symbolic force—they are at leisure to enjoy specially reserved areas of natural island beauty, while they are served by formally-clad and deferential Jamaicans. Of course, personal reactions to tourists by citizens of tourist areas are mixed, and usually fairly neutral or commercial. It is particularly at election time that anti-tourist feeling grows; it is a useful element in the political definition of the radical politician's constituency.

The effects of the huge migrations to Britain and North America are more difficult to judge, and they are clearly complex and sometimes contradictory. Some students may return embittered by metropolitan racialism, while others (or the same people) will use their achievements in the metropolis to validate their prestige at home. For the poorer Jamaicans, the migrations have obviously reduced the social distance between themselves and the whites and immigrant communities, and probably helped to undercut their feelings of solidarity in opposition to the traditional powers abroad and at home. Something of this feeling comes through in Louise Bennett's poem—

> Wat a joyful news, Miss Mattie,
> I feel like me heart gwine burs'
> Jamaica people colonizin
> Englan in reverse . . .
>
> Dem a-pour out o' Jamaica,
> Everybody future plan
> Is fe get a big-time job
> An settle in de mother lan.

Many of these developments have fed back into individual self-perception, and also into the ways in which others are evaluated. Symbolic assaults on the traditional structure have affected everybody. If one result has been the increased confidence and assertiveness of coloured and black Jamaicans, another has been the increasing insecurity of 'Jamaica whites' and Chinese Jamaicans, many of whom have chosen emigration. But while the cultural assertion of the urban poor has had remarkably little substantive political content, the fear of 'light' Jamaicans is often less of a racial Armageddon than of a 'Cuba' in Jamaica. (The nineteenth century fear of a 'Haiti' seems to have had stronger racial overtones.)

There is probably less agreement today than there was a generation ago as to the criteria for the evaluation of status, and there can be little doubt that these criteria are generally weighted differently today. The significance allowed to colour still varies from one group to another, and light-coloured people still tend to be most obsessed by it—in general they are the people who are careful not to get too tanned, whose women put their hair in curlers every day, and who are unhappy if their children marry people darker than themselves. The significance of colour also varies situationally. One may not be concerned with the colour of a business acquaintance or a colleague, but one tends to have friends of one's own class and general 'shade' (or 'complexion'). There are also odd reversals of sentiment, indicative of the current flux. For example, some coloured Jamaicans confess that they feel at a disadvantage because they are not racially 'pure' blacks. And as a white Jamaican academic pointed out to me, many people at the University who would have been stressing their light colour ten years ago, now call themselves blacks.

In studies of adolescent school-children, Dr Miller found that their ideal physical type, regardless of their own colour, was not Caucasian, but rather 'fair' or 'clear' skin colour associated with straight hair and a 'good' nose. This type was until recently favoured in beauty contests, great events in Jamaica, which often cause great controversy; but now there seems to be a bias in favour of choosing a darker contestant. Perhaps these preferences reflect the new power of the old, stereotypically 'brown' 'middle-class', and it is probably true that Dr Miller's subjects, and people whose voices count in beauty contests, are not representative of the Jamaican population as a whole. Indeed, Nettleford has suggested that contestants for international beauty competitions are selected with an eye to presenting a prestigious image of Jamaica, and that this involves choosing a light-coloured girl. In any case, these currents of opinion must be understood against a background in which colour values are even less straightforward than they were a generation ago, and probably considerably less significant.

Certain factors tend to perpetuate the colour complex in Jamaica. Some are endemic to the Jamaican political process, as I have indicated. Others are introduced by the fact that a racist model of white superiority remains entrenched in the metropolitan countries, though this too has been shaken in the past few years. But in Jamaica, over the last generation, the objective effects of colour on the life of individuals have been lessened. The last employment barriers have fallen, as dark people work in positions of visible trust in the banks, and nobody seriously argues that colour is a bar to employment or promotion.

To sum up, colour has ceased to be relevant to the legal status of Jamaicans, and one's colour is of very limited importance to one's career prospects. However, it continues to be a factor in political rhetoric, in self-image, and in the assessment of social status. But in all these areas colour, in the complex Jamaican sense, intermingles, as it has always done, with notions of style, general culture, and personal attitude. White and black, master and slave, England and Africa—the opposed pairs out of the past remain relevant in various situations, but they do not structure any by themselves.

There are deep historical roots for the peculiar development of

Jamaican racial attitudes. In the American South children of black and white parentage were classed 'Negro'. In South Africa a special, legally defined caste of 'Coloureds' was established. In Jamaica (and to varying degrees elsewhere in the Caribbean and Latin America) a different kind of development occurred. A permeable, ambiguous, coloured but free category developed into an interstitial but increasingly fuzzily defined section of the population, and so, at last, particularly when the end of the colonial political society was clearly at hand, it disappeared into a broader and even less sharply defined category, becoming, with people of diverse origins, part of the 'middle-class'. Thus the original, legally and racially defined strata, did not persist.

I have described the variety of folk-models which are built up on the basis of the shared, but ambiguous, racial symbols. There are also many 'multi-racial' contexts where the outstanding tendency is to talk an ideology of non-racialism, and this is true among all classes in the island. This is another of the competing models which Jamaicans sometimes use, and while it is difficult to assess the effects of ideological statements, it must be remembered that 'race' is a symbol, and thus vulnerable to symbolic and ideological assault. On the other hand, the countervailing tendency in some political circles to represent Jamaican society in terms of racial confrontation may take on a new edge in a period of serious economic recession, and then racial scapegoating may occur.

My objective in the last few chapters has been to delineate a coherent sociological approach to the general problem of social stratification in Jamaica. I have noted the great divide which exists between the mass of the poor and the small minority of the rich, but have been at pains to warn against the intellectual confusion which results from too gross a reliance upon this sort of distinction, or indeed upon any single measure which divides Jamaicans into distinct and contraposed blocs. On the contrary, I have stressed the significance of the contradictions which exist between various criteria of status, and the importance of regional, and situational variations in self-definition and the conception of the total society. These are not, I think, 'transitional' phenomena, but fundamental characteristics of modern Jamaica.

Chapter 15

The Two-party System

The most significant polarization of Jamaica's population is political, but paradoxically, this national split in political support is the most secure basis for the stability of the society. It is also the clearest evidence that Jamaica is not fundamentally split, into clearly-defined blocs, on the basis of social or economic criteria.

Roughly half the population supports the Peoples' National Party (PNP), while the other half supports the Jamaica Labour Party (JLP). This division, passionate and deeply-entrenched, is just thirty years old. It has no precedent in the country's history, and indeed it began only shortly after the introduction of adult suffrage in 1944.

Perhaps the oddest aspect of this situation, is that so many Jamaicans take it for granted. Yet of all the British colonies which became independent after the Second World War, only Jamaica, Barbados and Malta have maintained a working two-party system, in which there have been several peaceful and constitutional changes of government.[1] The very singular nature of Jamaica's political development has led some observers to question its stability. In particular, radical authors have argued that the mass of Jamaicans have been progressively alienated from the system, since they derive no rewards from it, and that in any case the racial and social tensions within the country will undermine the basic acceptance of the Jamaican political community. I shall discuss such questions in another chapter. My immediate purpose is to describe the two-party system and the pattern of party support.

Voting figures reflect the way in which the two-party system has become progressively more firmly entrenched (see Table 8). The outstanding tendency has been towards the elimination of independent and third-party candidates. From 1959 onwards

111

they have received a negligible proportion of the votes. In the first general election, in 1944, independents won 5 seats. In

TABLE 8   *Percentage of votes cast for parties at national elections*

Year	1944	1949	1955	1959	1962	1967	1972
JLP	41·4	42·7	39·3	44·3	50·0	50·7	42·9
PNP	23·5	43·5	50·5	54·8	48·6	49·1	56·1
Others	35·1	13·8	10·2	0·9	1·4	0·2	1·0

1949 they won two, but since then no candidate from outside the two major parties has won a parliamentary seat.[2] In 1962, the year of independence, 24 third-party and independent candidates presented themselves. They accounted for 21 per cent of the candidates in that election, but won, in all, only 1·4 per cent of the total vote. Millard Johnson and his PPP, fighting on a straightforward black racialist appeal, stood in 16 of the 45 seats then in contention, 8 of them in the Kingston metropolitan area. All their candidates forfeited their deposits.

This consolidation of electoral support behind the two main parties has been accompanied by a steady rise in the participation of registered voters in elections, as Table 9 shows.

TABLE 9   *Participation of registered voters in general elections (percentages)*

Year	1944	1949	1955	1959	1962	1967	1972
% voting	59	65	65	66	73	82	79

One observer attributed the slight decline in 1972 to the abstention of a number of disenchanted JLP voters, but he pointed out that participation was highest in marginal constituencies, a tribute to the political sophistication of the electorate.[3]

This steady rise in the turn-out of registered voters at elections is not, however, as significant as it might seem. Another factor must be taken into account. As a consequence of registration procedures, the size of the registered voter population has been subject to odd fluctuations. The JLP was in government from 1962 to 1972, and in this period the number of registered voters dropped from 797,000 in 1962 to 543,000 in 1967, rising only to

605,000 in 1972. The decrease was most marked in urban areas and among voters in their early 20s, and it was generally believed that the urban young would support the PNP opposition, which enjoyed a more radical image. There was also gerrymandering of constituencies. For example, the JLP government ensured that the three safe seats in St Thomas should be retained in 1972, although they had a total population of only 71,000, while the strong belt of PNP support in north St Andrew was contained within a single constituency with a population of 89,000.[4]

Despite such manipulation, historically practised by both parties, election results have provided a fair reflection of popular support. It is true that in 1949 the JLP won with a marginally smaller vote than the PNP, but in that election independents took nearly 14 per cent of the vote. The main effect of these manipulations has been to increase the yield of seats to the winning party, but in all two-party constituency systems the tendency is, in any case, for a small winning margin to be translated into a disproportionate majority of seats. The key fact is that swings in party support tend to be fairly even nationally. Moreover, no party dominates any region, and therefore however boundaries are drawn a swing against the government will be virtually impossible to disguise. Thus in 1967, with only 50·7 per cent of the vote to 49·1 per cent for the PNP, the JLP won 33 of the 53 seats in Parliament. However, despite energetic gerrymandering, the JLP shed 8 percentage points in 1972, winning only 42·9 per cent of the votes, and their share of the seats dropped to 16.

One might wonder why the manipulation of elections is not carried further by the party in government. Whatever the temptations might be, it would not appear to be practical politics. The reason is, first, that party support is distributed fairly evenly throughout the population. It is not concentrated in one particular racial, or regional, or class bloc, and so is not readily available for revolutionary action. The Burnham government in Guyana has maintained itself in power partly through such manipulation of the electoral rules, but this has been possible because of the fundamentally racial identity of the parties within a racially plural society. In contrast, the support of the Jamaican parties, as I shall show, is multi-racial and multi-class, and therefore not amenable to similar mobilization. A second reason

113

is the presence of a powerful middle-class, divided between the parties, and supporting a generally respected and non-political judiciary, which serves to maintain the constitutional provisions. Disputed elections are quickly brought to court, and fairly dealt with. Very recently a cabinet minister lost his parliamentary seat after a disputed result had been reviewed by the courts.

I do not think that the establishment of this two-party system in Jamaica has been accounted for satisfactorily, but part of the reason is perhaps to be found in historical accident. Jamaica was the first of the new wave of ex-colonies to be granted universal adult suffrage (in 1944), but one of the laggards in achieving full political independence (in 1962). The reasons for this lengthy periods of political tutelage are internal to Jamaican politics. The governor, Hugh Foot, was more impatient for full responsible government than were the political leaders.[5] In any case, the consequence was that the two major parties were able to institutionalize their positions as established rivals. Both also enjoyed periods in power. The JLP held office from 1944 to 1955. The PNP was in government from 1955 to 1962, when they lost a referendum in which they supported the incorporation of Jamaica in a West Indian Federation. The JLP won the subsequent election and led Jamaica into independence, losing again to the PNP, two elections later, in 1972. During the period between the establishment of democratic politics and national independence, then, the two parties were able to organize and to establish the rules of the political game, while the Governor held the ring.

It was also during this period of controlled political competition that the two parties established their monopoly at the polls, and built up their national support. The PNP began as a middle-class, white-collar and professional party. With the establishment of a party-backed union, the National Workers' Union (NWU) in 1952, they began to build up solid working-class support, and, at the time of independence, they even penetrated the lumpen-proletariat of Kingston, through a canny decision to treat seriously with the Rastafarians. The JLP began as a trade-union based populist movement, built around the charismatic figure of Alexander Bustamante, and in fact the union was called the Bustamante Industrial Trade Union (BITU). However, it attracted commercial allies as the PNP moved left (although the PNP purged its leading left-wingers in 1952). As the political system developed, so the parties became more similar. The PNP leader, Norman Manley, a distinguished lawyer, was forced to develop a popular touch and a concern with rough political tactics after the electoral defeats of 1944 and 1949, and the subsequent split in his party. The leader of the JLP, Manley's cousin Alexander Bustamante, was forced to rationalize his organization and policies after winning office. Thus by the time of independence the nature of the political competition itself had generated two moderate parties with mass, multi-class support.

The key point I wish to make is that support for one party or the other is not closely related to race, class, region or any obvious social indicator. To begin with, although the PNP was traditionally an urban party, there is not a very great difference in urban or rural support for either party, though there are significant areas of strength and weakness. In 1959, the PNP won 60 per cent of the urban votes and 52 per cent of the rural votes. In 1962, it won 52 per cent of the urban votes, while its share of the rural votes dropped slightly less, to 45 per cent.[6] In the following elections the PNP maintained its edge in the urban areas, but managed, particularly in 1972, to erode the support of the JLP in the northern and western constituencies, winning a majority of rural seats. JLP victories were concentrated in a belt of south-central and eastern constituencies.

None the less, it is clear from the election returns that no area of the country can be isolated as overwhelmingly JLP or PNP. This is shown by the large number of seats which change hands on a moderate electoral swing. Even in the 1972 PNP landslide, the party gained over 60 per cent of the votes in only 17 of the 53 seats, 5 being predominantly urban. The JLP took over 60 per cent of the votes in two constituencies, both urban. In that election, the PNP won 37 seats to 16 for the JLP. However, if an election were to be held again with the same constituencies, a 4 per cent swing against the government would give the JLP a majority.[7] As Mr Morrissey remarked, comparing the 1967 and 1972 election returns:[8]

> it is clear that the relative rankings of constituencies
> changed little between the two General Elections, confirming
> the author's contention that there was a fairly even 'swing'
> in political allegiance throughout the country, and hence

the loss by the JLP of all constituencies with a small 'safety margin'. Jamaican voters again behaved in the remarkably uniform manner observed by Faber with regard to the 1962 Election.

If the country is regionally fairly evenly divided between the parties, the evidence suggests that social classes are equally politically balanced. The rural constituencies are made up of an overwhelming majority of smallholders and rural labourers, and the labourers are themselves concentrated in constituencies near the coast, where the large estates are generally found. The balance in rural constituencies therefore reflects a split in this class between the parties. There is less evidence for affiliation of the rural middle-class, but in the area I studied this was also evenly split, except for the school-teachers who were solidly behind the PNP.[9] The pattern of support in Kingston has been more systematically investigated by Dr Stone.

Stone questioned a stratified sample survey of urban residents in Kingston and St Andrew, and found that 50 per cent had always voted PNP, while 35 per cent had always voted for the JLP, and 15 per cent had voted for both parties. Thus party preference was strongly fixed for the majority of voters, and the strength of this attachment varied little with social class. He cross-tabulated partisan preference with occupational categories and found that (a) all his 'classes' were fundamentally divided between the parties, although (b) his business respondents were biased

TABLE 10 *Cross-tabulation of occupational categories and partisan preference*[11]

| | Percentage of sample favouring | | | |
	PNP	JLP	Independent	Anti-party
1 Business	19	71	10	0
2 Professional	40	37	20	3
3 Small businessmen	47	43	0	10
4 White-collar	60	16	16	8
5 Self-employed artisan	59	14	13	14
6 Blue-collar, working-class	38	29	12	11
7 Lower-class	28	41	10	31
8 Total	45	31	13	11

towards the JLP, while white-collar workers and artisans tended to favour the PNP, and (c) a significant minority of the poor unemployed in the city rejected both parties.[10]

Stone does not tell us what proportion of the sample was made up by each category, but it appears that at the one extreme blue-collar workers comprised 38 per cent of the sample, while, at the other extreme, upper-class and upper-middle-class individuals comprised only 3 per cent. This may reflect actual distributions of these categories in the population, but it means that his sample for some categories must have been very small. In the absence of tests of significance, therefore, one must hesitate in attributing great significance to the biases within the big business category. Similar considerations may apply in the case of the other divergent categories, the white-collar workers and self-employed artisans. It is noteworthy that the two largest groups, the lowest two occupational levels, are divided into two large blocs. If one takes urban 'blue-collar and working-class' and 'lower class' together, they appear to be evenly divided between the two parties. The criteria used in dividing these two levels are unclear in Stone's account, and even in the form in which he has presented the evidence, it is difficult to accept the strength of his argument that the PNP is basically an alliance of the solid middle-class and the upper-working-class strata, while the JLP brings together the upper-class with the lowest class of the working population. These occupational categories are not shown to be self-conscious interest groups, and in any case they are quite clearly divided between the parties. Leaving aside the 'big business' category, which must have been minuscule in the sample, and taking into account the vague boundary between the two lowest categories, the only significant divergence appears to be the bias of the white-collar workers and self-employed artisans in favour of the PNP. Stone's conclusions are further weakened by the failure to take into account the rural vote. If the parties are to be analysed as class-coalitions, then the rural interest must be taken into account. In fact such an analysis is bound to fail. A comparison with democracies in which there are stable class-based parties points up the lack of correlation in Jamaica between the parties and any one class, or coalition of classes.[12]

There remains the possibility that the parties are racially divided. Of course the overwhelming majority of Jamaicans are black and working-class, or rural labourers and small farmers, and they are fairly evenly divided between the parties. The so-called 'brown' Jamaicans, found in all classes but particularly prominent in middle-class occupations, are also obviously divided, although to the extent that white-collar workers may be disproportionately 'brown', there may be a tendency (suggested by some writers) for this category to favour the PNP. This would not be a particularly powerful identification, however, although it is sometimes played upon by opponents of the PNP. The ethnic minorities and the tiny 'white' Jamaican group are less easily classified, for there is little data to go on. All provide prominent financial backers and members of both parties, and my fieldwork in Westmoreland showed that the Indian estate workers and middle-class there did not introduce ethnic considerations in their political choices, even when one candidate was an Indian. One must conclude, then, that 'race', like region and occupation is not a good guide to political inclination.

Dr Stone's data from Kingston supports this argument. Among the white-collar workers in his sample, he found that 'browns' divided 65 per cent for the PNP and 11 per cent for the JLP, while 'blacks' were 59 per cent PNP and 20 per cent JLP. Among blue-collar and working-class respondents, 'browns' were 56 per cent PNP and 28 per cent JLP, while 'blacks' were 45 per cent PNP and 43 per cent JLP. As he says, these results show 'a moderately higher pro-PNP tendency among both the white collar and blue collar, brown respondents'. However one must dispute his conclusion that this reinforces his thesis 'of the entrenched middle class symbolism of the PNP'.[13] Even if one accepts (and I do not) that 'brown' and 'middle-class' are 'symbolically' interchangeable in Jamaica, the tendencies are too slight to be of great interest—certainly in the continued absence of tests of statistical significance. Once again, the Jamaican situation appears most clearly in contrast to other political systems where ethnicity and race really are important bases of party-support, as in Guyana, Trinidad, or even parts of the USA.

I have shown that to a very large degree political-party support in Jamaica is independent of such social factors as class, 'race', or region. This does not mean that it is simply a random matter. Communities in town and country often tend to be solidly identified with one party or the other, and there are a couple of local party machines which have succeeded in creating local strongholds. Moreover, immediate self-interest may be determined by membership of a particular union (for the two major unions are adjuncts of the two parties, and a union member is expected to be a party-supporter), or by the belief that particular jobs will be given to the supporters of a particular party. This may be because the party controls a local government council, which employs many people, or a Land Authority, which provides loans, etc. However, as Stone's figures suggest, and as the general assumptions of Jamaicans confirm, party-support is remarkably stable and is not easily shaken by sudden reversals in local party fortunes.

This brings me to my final point, which is that most voters support the party of their choice with considerable fervour. Choices may be made for a variety of reasons, not closely related to national policies, particularly since these are differently presented and evaluated by articulate politicians. Nevertheless, once the choices are made they are given enormous emotional weight. Friendships may be broken over politics, even families divided. Party-posters, photographs of leaders, etc. are commonly used to decorate homes and shops, and political debate is usually highly-charged, and, at election time, often violent. An experience of my own may illustrate this. When I first began fieldwork in D . . . I explained that I was working for the government. Since the PNP had recently come to power, people assumed that I must therefore be a strong 'PNP-ite'. Nobody seemed to mind that I was foreign, well-educated, or light in colour. The key barrier to friendship with most local people was my presumed political affiliation. On the other hand, it opened all doors with others, mainly in neighbouring districts, who supported the PNP. It was not that government personnel were regarded as remote and dangerous figures, as is commonly the case in developing countries. On the contrary, if I came from *their* government I was one of them; if not, of course, not.

The degree of emotional attachment suggests that people identify with the party of their choice in a very personal sense. This is not a consequence of a party being identified with, say, 'black' people, or manual workers, or small farmers, since such identifications are not present. Nor are policy differences in the usual sense the cause of these attachments, since policies are not

119

clearly articulated by either party, except on specific issues, which are often temporary, or of a technical nature. Identification is rather with the individual leaders of the party, at the national level in particular, and with the traditional image of the party.

Both parties are regarded in part as the expression of the personalities of their founders, the cousins Norman Manley and Alexander Bustamante. Both hero-figures, larger than life, trailed immense personal myths of strength, courage and achievement. The present leaders, Michael Manley, son of Norman, and his distant relative ('cousin') Shearer, who is in turn fictive 'son' of Bustamante, are also the subject of endless local myths celebrating their sexual, intellectual and manly attributes. Other leaders are sometimes treated in a similar way, and indeed hero-worship, and identification with heroes, is a marked feature of Jamaican culture. Membership of either party, then, implies the possibility of association or even identification with a hero.

Other aspects of party image may also generate emotional attachment. The JLP is, its name implies, the party of 'labour'. It is thus my party, since I labour. The PNP is the party of intellectuals, educated men, and so of intelligent men like me. On the obverse side, the JLP cabinet after ten years in power was accused of corruption and factionalism. *They* are dishonest and divided. The PNP has been haunted by a Red smear, and in some eyes a few PNP leaders have been too eager to assert 'African' loyalties. *They* are reds and racialists.

In other words, in the absence of ideological differences, or clear representation of special interests, the parties are none the less structured in such a way as to encourage emotional attachment. Yet there is little in the party myths which would be likely to determine anyone's choice of allegiance. The myths operate rather to justify and reinforce a choice which has been made, and they are structurally identical. At the same time, the composition of the two parties is very similar, and it would be difficult to say more about their general policies than that the PNP tends to include some radicals. I believe that the most important determinant of political support in Jamaica is, in the end, the ability of the leaders to enthuse their supporters. The personality of individual leaders is crucial, and they can also very largely shape party policy.

Chapter 16

Middle-class Leadership

If the two parties recruit substantial numbers of members at every social and occupational level, the leadership of both can be roughly described as 'middle-class'. People with political in-influence are generally educated and respectable, Jamaican-born and raised, professional and business people. A few have emerged from less predictable occupations, particularly within the trade union movement, but as their political influence has grown so, by style, contacts, and attitudes, they have tended to adjust to the orientations of their political peers. One might almost talk of a political class, since people of this sort are generally organized in various ways which allow them to bring political pressure to bear on the party leadership.

The leading figures in commerce and industry maintain active 'chambers', which make widely-publicized statements on a great range of government policies, and have considerable influence in determining middle-class judgments of government policy. Business leaders combine with the professionals in the 'service clubs' which are such a feature of modern Jamaica. These clubs (Rotary, Jaycees, Lions, etc.), like their American counterparts, serve both as a leisure and charity organization and as a means of crystallizing the opinions of their members on national issues. Speeches at such clubs by politicians, diplomats and businessmen are often publicized in the press and on radio and television. There are also professional organizations and old-boy associations which bring together influential men and serve as bases for the formulation and expression of specific political demands.

Professional and business people in Jamaica probably make up less than 10 per cent of the population, however broadly one wishes to define this national pool of influential and respected people. I exclude from this category expatriates and the remnants of the

121

plantocracy, for they have little direct political influence on politicians or the general public. This would mean that perhaps 30,000 men rank as potential men of influence, on the most liberal count. Most of them were educated in a handful of grammar schools, which link them in loyal cliques even as ageing men, and they are further organized in the network of clubs and associations I have described. These figures are approximate—mere guesses—for there is no study of the Jamaican political élite, but it is probably near enough for present purposes. The point I wish to make is simply that the pool of influential men is not large nationally, and that it is fairly homogeneous, and organized in a number of voluntary associations. Members of this category will be familiar with others in it, at least by name or reputation, or by some contact with their family. I believe, further, that every member of this category has the possibility of personal contact, through no more than one intermediary, with a member of the cabinet, or a leading member of the opposition.

In order to understand how political influence is monopolized by people in this category, it is necessary to look briefly at the organization of the political parties. Every party division is led by a more or less formal committee, including the member of parliament or parliamentary candidate. There are also local, less formal, centres of organization, led often by the local government councillors. These leaders are people in middle-class occupations, who have access to political favours, particularly those controlled by local councils or Land Authorities.

Dr Robertson has studied the membership of such local party branches by means of a (rather small) national sample. Of 169 voters sampled, 45 (27 per cent) said that they were party members, although only 35 (21 per cent) had paid their party dues. He found that very few of the paid-up party members had anything to do with selecting candidates. Moreover political awareness, or at least information, was not significantly higher among party members than among their peers. Robertson stressed that the parties were not ideological, mobilizing movements, and that members were interested in winning direct personal benefits.[1] In fact the local party branch is less a policy-making body, or a candidate-selecting machine, than a means of translating patronage into organized and reliable support. I found that there tend to be two or three highly-motivated members drawn from the lower social categories, who work closely with local leaders to organize communities on a narrow, local basis, for elections.

There appear to be a large number of local political blocs, based on effective communities, which tend to support one party on a community basis. Such blocs are often bounded by equivalent blocs supporting the other party, and in some areas such units form a patchwork quilt across the countryside. Perhaps communal rivalries are finding expression in rival affiliations, while the identity of the effective community is maintained and expressed by political solidarity. [2]

Considering the rural areas first, I found (and so did Dr Foner) that a crucial factor in the formation of such local attachments is the influence exercised by individual members of the local gentry or middle-class, who compete with each other, through the media of favours, treats, the invocation of local loyalties, and so forth.

These rural men and women who enjoy local influence are generally divided into two competing networks, each attached to one party. It is virtually impossible for any prominent rural citizen to remain neutral. If he tries he is none the less assigned a party loyalty by general gossip. I was amazed to find, also, that highly-educated rural leaders sometimes believed that the local party boss *knew* how they voted at the polls, although there can be no question but that the ballot is effectively secret.

Immediate self-interest is not always a good guide to political affiliation in this class. Even taking the most cynical view, one must remember that the parties alternate in power, and are expected to continue to do so, and that therefore there is a belief that loyalty will be rewarded. Moreover, even if one's party is out of power nationally, it may control the parish council, or at least return one's local councillor, and so a loyal party member may retain some access to favours even at times of low party fortune. Choice of party allegiance is therefore often influenced by personal accidents, such as the relationship a person or his family may have with party leaders, the views of one's wife's family or close friends, and so on. Changes in such circumstances may lead to a change of affiliation, as may the offer of a great personal advantage, but among such leading figures loyalty is highly regarded, and a man may sacrifice too much in the way of general respect if he is seen to make a cynical switch of party affiliation. Certainly he could not do this more than once. Finally, friendship networks tend to be uni-party, and a man who abandons his party will often lose his friends.

In short, local political leadership is in the hands of two competing networks of well-off and respected friends, and they compete for the support of the mass of the rural population, through patronage and the use of local, community-based loyalties. It is to them that the national politicians must look, and it is their views they must take into account.

The urban working-class areas are not always amenable to this kind of organization. In some a professional politician has managed to build-up a community-based 'Tammany' operation, through the use of patronage, and, fairly commonly, some intimidation by gangs of youths. There are three such political bases in Kingston, all led by ministers or former ministers, and all situated in areas of the city where there are solid, native-Kingstonian populations.

More generally, however, the working-class is provided with a central political organization through the trade unions. At this point, a slight digression is necessary on the subject of the Jamaican trade unions, for they are peculiar in organization and of great political significance.

In 1960 an observer noted, 'It is already a truism of Jamaican politics that successful competition for mass electoral support cannot be achieved by a party without a well-organized trade union base'.[3] Each of the major parties is integrally associated with a trade union, and no party could possibly succeed in Jamaica without such an association. On the other hand, the political history of Jamaica shows that a trade union without a political-party is unlikely to be virile and powerful. Moreover, the monopoly of the parties, and of the unions (for the TUC is now a tolerated ally of the NWU) makes it extremely difficult for competitors to organize. In such situations the unions have sometimes agreed on a truce in order to freeze out the upstart.

The key role of the unions is reflected in the tendency for access to party leadership to be restricted to trade union leaders. The successors of Bustamante in the JLP, Sangster and Shearer, both came up through positions of leadership in the party union, the BITU. In the PNP, Norman Manley was succeeded by his son, but not in a simple act of inheritance. He was strongly challenged by a party 'star', and a major factor in his success was his position as Island Supervisor of the NWU.

To a large extent the union is the main support of the opposition party, and it benefits to some degree from opposition. The union of the governing party may be somewhat inhibited from taking radical action, and its leadership may be sapped by governmental tasks. The opposition, on the contrary, can allow its union a free hand. The competition between the unions, and their political dimension, are unquestionably costly in economic terms. Politically, however, the balance between them is a major source of the stability of the system.

The individual worker in an industry, or on a site, where union representation is arranged, is perforce a member of the union. Indeed, he may have got his job only through union membership, for local organizers can persuade employers that industrial peace will be more easily maintained if they are given a say in the selection of unskilled workers. Union membership provides clear and concrete material advantages. It is also presumed, by the union organizers, and, in general, by members, to imply support for the appropriate party. Although the union does not cover all of the urban workers, and in rural areas is a factor only on the estates and mining centres, it does provide a vital means for the organization of the poorer Jamaicans, particularly where local community-based organizations are lacking.

The leaders of the unions have always been professional or at any rate middle-class men, with strong political interests. Union leadership tends to be, in Jamaica, a special form of professional political activity, and union leaders are often promoted into leading political offices.

Thus the organized worker is represented by middle-class trade union leaders, and his demands are formulated only with respect to employment, wages, and working conditions. For various reasons, the unions do not formulate policies on education, welfare, general economic strategies, etc. They do not, in short, formulate general working-class demands, but simply work-related demands.

The broader aspirations of the workers and other poorer Jamaicans may be channelled through politicians or local political leaders, but normally these are formulated as particular 'favours' and negotiated through a patronage link. The churches once served as an effective pressure-group for the poor, but they no longer do so. Perhaps this is a consequence of the localization of the clergy, now themselves in general members of the local establishment. In short, the only effective channels of communication from the working-class to the government are via individual men of influence. In general, therefore, their demands are inferred by leaders, rather than formulated in general terms by organizations.

Thus the central condition of the Jamaican political process is this: a member of the middle-class (or at least a man of substance) can press a demand directly via nearly equal intermediaries, and if his demand is shared by many of his peers, it can be pressed by effective organizations. A poor Jamaican can only hope that a man of influence will take up his 'case' as a special favour. This does not necessarily mean that his broader demands will never be considered; but if they are, they will depend upon the influence of individual radical politicians, and the party's perception of the tactical situation.

POSTSCRIPT: In 1974, Mr Edward Seaga was elected to the leadership of the JLP in succession to Mr Shearer. A former Minister of Finance, and of 'Syrian' extraction, Mr Seaga's power base is not the BITU, but rather the party organization and his strategic Kingston constituency, the poor, turbulent but well-organized Tivoli Gardens.

Chapter 17

Policy-making

The political process can be viewed as a decision-making process. Centrally-placed authorities, enjoying suitable support, can make decisions for which there is a strategically placed demand, according to conventions which are institutionalized. The figure attempts to specify the relevant categories of people, offices and institutions involved in the formulation and processing of political demands in Jamaica.

The specification of the interest groups and their spokesmen is fairly straightforward, and follows from my earlier analysis. I have distinguished the political interests of foreign governments, various capitalists organizations, and other, internal interest-groups. I have also included the rural and urban poor, for the sake of completeness. In practice their views are not expressed through a special organization but rather inferred by politicians and other leaders of opinion, with an eye to vote-winning, or the avoidance of possible disruption. Each organized interest group uses appropriate channels of communication, both to press their views on politicians and to mobilize broader support for their demands.

The right-hand side of the figure may need more comment. The people actually responsible for the formulation of policy are, constitutionally, the politicians. In practice, however, the senior civil servants can formulate decisions in the interstices of the politicians' policies, which may cumulatively amount almost to a distinct policy. They can also often interpret political decisions in a fairly flexible way, or, by neglecting or delaying certain actions, effectively undermine a political decision. That is why I have drawn an arrow showing political decisions of the cabinet being subject to modification by top civil servants before emerging as effective policies.

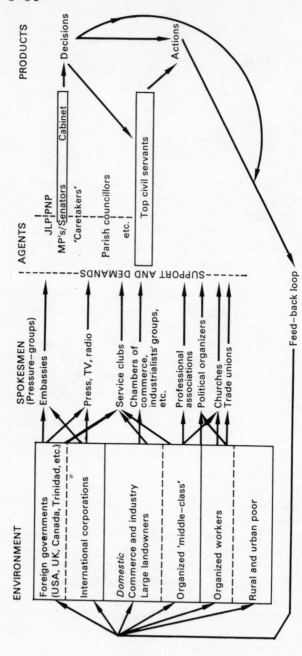

The Jamaican political process

I have suggested that the politically-crucial demands are those of 'middle-class' Jamaicans. This crude statement demands modification. To begin with, Jamaicans of all classes are divided between the parties, and to a certain extent a section of the more influential party-supporters will swallow a policy if they believe it to be necessary to ensure the success of the party. They will in any case be more favourably disposed to initiatives, even radical initiatives, which come from their own party leaders. Second, this 'middle-class' is not homogeneous, or made up of people with clearly formulated demands. To a very great extent, the most general political demands are shared by the majority of Jamaicans, and controversial policies do not split the country on class lines. None the less, people whom one would broadly regard as 'middle-class', and who would be likely to accept such a designation, do share a particular interest in low taxation, a minimum of government intervention in commerce, and, in general, the protection of private property rights.

Jamaican businessmen are particularly well-organized to press their demands, but their interests are not always congruent with those of the most powerful economic bodies, the multi-national corporations. They, with their monopolistic positions, are most concerned with predictability, with maintaining control of the long-term development of their operations. They are in direct competition with local business only with respect to labour, where they pursue their own policies which are not uniform. The bauxite companies have set the top limits on the wage-scales, and have created new and formerly undreamt-of aspirations for the workers. They have also worked closely with the unions, and greatly strengthened them in consequence. The sugar companies set the bottom level of the wage-scales, and have inhibited the development of a modern rural work-force. The distinctness of these economic interests is reflected in the generally contented attitude adopted by Jamaican capitalists when, recently, the PNP government turned the screws on the bauxite companies. This policy also showed up the weakness of the international corporations, given the modern 'low-profile' favoured by American diplomacy, particularly at the nadir of Richard Nixon's presidency. The major sugar concerns had anticipated that their position would become increasingly weak, and have rid themselves of their land-holdings, selling them to the government.

The way in which these various configurations of interest and power manifest themselves in decision-making is best revealed through a consideration of particular instances. I shall first consider a recent attempt to impose a new land tax.

Under the previous, JLP, government, there was widespread concern with the level of agricultural production, and the government initiated a register of idle lands. The idea was that once this was completed, it could be used for administrative action designed to bring idle lands into production. Perhaps some of this land would even be redistributed. On 2 May 1973, Michael Manley, the new PNP Prime Minister, announced that a levy would be imposed on landowners whose lands were not in full production. This did not appear at first to be a radically new initiative, although the JLP administration had taken no steps once the register of idle lands had laboriously been compiled. However, the announcement of the new tax set off a furore.

The *Daily Gleaner* solemnly editorialized about the uncertainty afflicting the business community after the announcement of the land tax in insufficient detail, together with other budget proposals (4 May 1973). A week later the paper reported that an emergency meeting of the Associated Chambers of Commerce of Jamaica had been called to discuss the new 'Property Tax'; and it explained that this meeting would be the climax of a series of public and private meetings of various Chambers and special committees set up across the country. On 14 May another editorial stressed the damaging uncertainty about the provisions, which was causing 'mounting concern in every sector of the economy'. The Chamber of Commerce called on the government to suspend the land tax, and Mr Seaga, a leading figure in the JLP, suggested that the government's move was just one aspect of a vast land-acquisition spree, which would soon be aimed at the bauxite companies. He told a US Businessmen's Luncheon Club at the Sheraton Hotel that 'the farmer will have to sell since he cannot pay the penal tax' (*Daily Gleaner*, 17 May 1973).

As the uproar mounted, the government wavered. In the first place, it seems that the civil service had not worked out the details of the tax before the announcement was made, so that ministers tended to flounder when challenged on detailed repercussions. Second, the purpose of the tax was left a little obscure. On 17 May, the Prime Minister suggested that it would pay for the new free education provisions of the budget, but this was later denied. However, on 20 May the Minister of Finance began a reasoned counter-offensive, with a long statement on radio and television, which went some way towards placating the *Daily Gleaner's* editorialist. He followed this up with a meeting with representatives of the business community, who expressed some reassurance. The government also introduced de-rating procedures, a new time-scale for the collection of the tax, and an appeal system for 'special cases'. Effectively, the policy was largely emasculated.

It is worth quoting the account of the *Gleaner* columnist, 'William Strong' (*Daily Gleaner*, 30 May 1973):

Within hours after Finance Minister David Coore had announced new property taxes for the 1973–4 fiscal year, public opinion was ablaze throughout the country. Within days common interest groups coalesced in public interest (sic), sparking new groups of protesters into action. Never in Jamaican history was any Government so bombarded, so quickly and completely.

There seemed no single citizen left anywhere (sic) who was not funnelling his protest to Government through some group channel. Long-established organisations of every type, long dormant ones, and others born overnight sprung into action to join the mass protest. There was no half-heartedness about their protests either; they were organized, aroused, determined that the new tax proposal, though acceptable in principle, was totally unacceptable in application as it foretold the ruin of all landowners and therefore should be rethought out.

Facing such a solid wall of public opinion, Government applied reasonableness, and gave both clarification and reassurances. In one vital respect, the Government backtracked. But as quickly as was possible, Government took the menace out of the tax.

This columnist is not regarded as anti-PNP, and his comments spare the government in a way which a JLP writer would not have done. However, the key omission in this review is, of course, the recognition that the tax involved only large holders of land. The putative beneficiaries were not organized and brought no direct pressure to bear.

To sum up, a rational tax measure, rooted in a long-standing bipartisan policy to increase agricultural productivity, and to reduce the holding of idle land for speculation, was largely defeated through a concerted movement of protest, including diverse land-holding and business groups. They successfully won general 'middle-class' support, via the network of middle-class organizations and clubs. With the support of the press, they represented the tax as part of an assault upon private property, and as a danger to 'the farmer' in particular. The government made no attempt to organize a counter-pressure from small farmers, who might be allowed to work some of the idle land, or from urban workers whose food-bills might be affected as a consequence of greater agricultural productivity.

This process was repeated at the same time with respect to two other proposals in the same budget, one extending free education to the secondary level, and the other imposing a tax on work-permits granted to foreign workers. In both cases the original proposals were greatly whittled down, and, again, organized middle-class opinion was mobilized, and the assault was directed at the wide areas of ambiguity in the proposals. No outsider can hope to establish the crucial reason for this characteristic ambiguity. It may have arisen through disagreement in the cabinet, imperfectly resolved, or the obfuscation of civil servants, or sheer incompetence.

I do not wish to suggest, however, that propertied interests simply manipulate broader 'middle-class' groups and successfully override government initiatives. Opposition politicians are always interested in challenging government policy, and may be as active in their purely political interest as any interest-group with concrete economic benefits at risk. Moreover, the fervour of the debate was a consequence partly of the widespread fear, among all sections of the rural population, as well as among the business and professional classes, that the moves presaged a general radical reorientation of the country, which would let in 'Castroism'. A consideration of another issue, 'law and order', may help to indicate the importance of non-material interests.

Dr Stone has nicely demonstrated the relationship between the incidence of theft, larceny and robbery, and unemployment in

Jamaica between 1947 and 1970. The relationship is very close,[1] although there was a shift towards greater use of guns in the 1960s, partly, it has been suggested, because American interests repay suppliers of marijuana with guns, partly, others suggest, because some urban politicians armed their followers. I do not think that either explanation is very convincing, but the fact is that violent crime came to be regarded as a major problem in Jamaica. Studies of crime in Jamaica are virtually non-existent, but it was popularly believed that the rise in violent crime reflected the hostility, indiscipline and racialism of the urban dispossessed, and that it represented not only a threat to individual security, but in some way a threat to the state itself. Certainly it was a challenge to any government.

The PNP government began, in 1972, with a liberal position on law enforcement. The Minister of Home Affairs and Justice took an early opportunity to tell the House that harsh penalties alone were not a solution, and he opposed mandatory sentences which the opposition favoured. In particular, a much more lenient view was taken of marijuana offences, which had been very severely punished under the JLP administration, and many minor offenders were released from prison. The Minister also tried to introduce measures which would reduce the private ownership of firearms, although the *Daily Gleaner* editorialist warned that in his view, 'the fewer guns in the hands of law-abiding citizens the higher will be the incidence of crimes such as house-breaking and burglary' (30 August 1972).

The general reaction to these measures was unfavourable, and soon police activity was stepped up in slum areas. In November the Prime Minister declared a 'war to the death' on 'gunmen'. The opposition was still making capital over the continuance of violent crime, and violent offences were now given enormous publicity. In December the Prime Minister retaliated by suggesting that criminals were linked with 'subversive elements', and he later made it clear that he meant that some leaders of the JLP were in cahoots with criminals to embarrass the government. A former JLP minister complained about the indiscriminate searches to which the city's poor were being subjected, but this issue did not find favour.

The anti-crime policy was pressed forward, with sudden and violent joint army–police raids on slum areas. During a few

months of 1973 there were almost daily reports in the press of
'gunmen' being shot 'attacking the police' or 'resisting arrest'.
A commentator remarked on the Jamaica Broadcasting Corpora-
tion that the police were executing more Jamaicans than the public
hangman, and he was banned from the air, with general public
approval. Reports like these became common (*Daily Gleaner*, 17
June 1973):

> Three men, including a gang leader, were killed, five guns
> seized and over 50 persons taken into custody during
> police/military operations yesterday. Two men were also
> hospitalised with gunshot wounds sustained in incidents
> involving the police and military.
> Yesterday's toll resulted from several clashes between the
> police and military on the one hand and wanted men and
> suspects on the other.

The next day, 'The police shot and killed a man who reportedly
attacked them with a machete when they swooped down on a
suspected ganja den late Saturday night' (*Daily Gleaner*, 18 June
1973). And on the next day (*Daily Gleaner*, 19 June 1973),

> A burglar was shot dead and another held when the police
> surprised them at a gas station on the Red Hills Road early
> yesterday morning.
> The slain burglar, who according to the police had
> attacked them with a crowbar, was identified as. . . .

And so it went on.

In June the House of Representatives approved tougher
penalties for the possession of guns which had not been licensed,
but the Minister of Home Affairs, reversing his previous stand,
now urged the public to 'prepare and train yourself to use the gun,
and once you draw don't be too slow because the other chap may
be younger, his reflexes may be fast' (*Daily News*, 19 June 1973).
On this occasion the *Daily News* demurred, but a month later,
reading the public mood rather better, it called in a leader for
'drastic action to combat crime'. The drive against criminals
was all to the good, 'But criminals in Jamaica today are like the

heads of the Hydra—for each one that is caught two more spring up to take his place.' And they called for drastic action 'beyond the authority of the police' (*Daily News*, 18 July 1973). In the same month the Prime Minister announced draconian new measures, and, coming full circle from his original position, told the nation on television that 'If ganja leads to guns both must be fought equally' (*Daily Gleaner*, 27 July 1973). A new and more active Minister of Home Affairs was appointed, and his first task was to organize the new 'Gun Courts', special courts set up in the military barracks in Kingston, which were to pass indeterminate sentences on anyone possessing firearms or ammunition without a licence.

There is no question but that Jamaica in the past few years has suffered from a high level of violent crime. How high is difficult to determine, in the absence of sophisticated studies, nor is the tendency at all obvious. Nevertheless, the hysteria reflected in the policies and actions of the short period reviewed above cannot be regarded as rational responses to the situation. It was never established that there were organized gangs of substance; certainly, despite the regular police/army raids none was ever uncovered. Nor were the links, suggested by the Prime Minister, between criminals and opposition politicians, although there must have been a special inducement to reveal these had they existed. Connections with American gangsters, the existence of a 'Mr Big', etc. were all widely talked-of, but never demonstrated. It seems rather more likely that no such basis for crime existed.

It is more reasonable to see the whole business as a witch-hunt. All the elements are there—the hysteria, the wild rumours and charges, all tending to suggest the existence of a secret and powerful group challenging the established order; the violent and indiscriminate counteraction. Of course, there was a lot of crime; but then, somehow, however many men were killed in the slums, crime went on. The Rastafarians might once have been more openly identified as the criminal element, and many police and army personnel certainly made this identification; but by the 1970s the Rastafarians were too well known, they had lost most of their terrors.

With the establishment of the gun-court, passions began to fall. Some respectable citizens were caught with ammunition or guns, and imprisoned; one was arrested after calling the police to his house to investigate a theft. The legal profession expressed its disapproval with the new court and the new laws, and the opposition tentatively began to try a civil liberties line. Crimes of violence were now reported without much drama, and police/military operations came to a stop.

This was not a class-war. It was a national movement against the eternal, threatening outsider, and the capitulation of the government to the hysteria is the more notable in that it overrode the challenges which came from the most respected quarter of middle-class opinion, the legal profession and the judiciary. It was not a factional war either, although there were moments when it seemed that it might take such a turn. The people who paid the price of the hysteria were little men in the slums, sometimes no doubt petty criminals, sometimes perhaps real gangsters. But even in the slums, the hysteria could be heard, reflected in the views of the older men and women in particular. Of course, any nation can be united in a religious war, and this does not mean that its people have many political ideas in common. But in this case, the witch-hunt reflected (and developed) the common feeling that 'our' island and way-of-life were threatened by a sinister force, which everyone could unite to oppose.

In conclusion, I shall briefly recapitulate the main features of Jamaica's political system. There is strong popular involvement in politics, and a high rate of participation in elections. The two parties, together, monopolize electoral support, and each enjoys a multi-class following. Electoral choices, and policies developed by government, clearly reflect the dominant influence of established business and professional groups.

These are the parameters of the system. A government must aim at winning popular support at the next election, but it must recognize that this support is partly mediated by influential middle-class leaders. No government can afford to alienate the vociferous and organized members of the business and professional classes. Thus parties must balance between the need to appeal to the mass of the population, and the danger of alienating influential men. The normal tactic is to appeal to the general population mainly through symbolic gestures, while actually delivering only those material advantages which the established interests will tolerate. If there seems to be a danger of the balance favouring the poorer elements at the expense of the more privileged (normally during a PNP administration), then the constraints begin rapidly to materialize. The middle-class clubs begin an agitation, rumours fly, money begins to be salted away in Miami, foreign investors indicate that they will wait before they invest again, and civil servants adopt postures of passive resistance. These processes are naturally enthusiastically supported by the opposition party.

On the other hand, there are factors which prevent any government from merely pandering to the privileged. First of all, the opposition party and its union will make capital out of such policies, increasing support for its union, and probably swinging to its side much uncommitted support among the poor. Second, the established middle-class, and many political leaders, have a profound fear of the possibility of popular riots, which had such an impact at the end of the 1930s, and which have occurred sporadically since. There is also a feeling that the widespread poverty in the country shames all Jamaicans, and must be ameliorated.

Chapter 18

Political Mobilization and Social Change

I have now completed my description of the transformation of modern Jamaica: the economic and demographic developments, the changes in social consciousness, the emergence of the new political structure have been outlined, and some of the links between these processes have been discussed. If the analysis has selected the appropriate variables, and understood them correctly, then it should be possible to say something about the future of Jamaica.

The major innovation in my analysis has been the refusal to depend upon a simple stratification model of Jamaica, and this is also my starting-point in looking forward to the future. I arrived at this point of view through a progressive understanding of the sources of Jamaican social science, and of the fluidity of Jamaican social classifications. However, after completing the analysis I came upon a recent essay by Lloyd Fallers, which made the general theoretical point far better than I could have done:[1]

> what are often called 'objective' inequalities—inequalities
> of wealth and power—can be understood only in their
> cultural contexts—only in the context of their *meaning* to
> those involved in them. Simply to chart the distribution
> of some 'objective' attribute—say income or education—on a
> diagram with arbitrarily fixed intervals is harmless enough
> and even useful, if all one wants to know is the distribution
> of income or education—both important aspects of
> inequality. . . . If education and material income mean
> different things in different human communities, still one
> learns something, in a rough, first-approximation sort of
> way, by comparing them in these terms. Difficulties arise,

however, when the classes are seen as sociocultural classes or strata—when, that is, it is whole persons or groups or roles that are portrayed in a vertical, layer-cake distribution, for this implies a great deal more about a society and its culture than can be safely assumed arbitrarily from an external observer's standpoint. The very use of a vertical dimension implies meanings—evaluative standards and cognitive images in terms of which a society's members, individually and in groups, perceive and evaluate (or grant deference to) one another—in short it implies a *culture* of inequality. Furthermore, by portraying a whole society in a single image, it implies *a* culture of inequality—a particular set of cognitive images and evaluative standards— an implication which denies our common knowledge that in every society, even the 'simplest', there is social differentiation—a division of labour—and that culture is to some extent differentiated into sub-culture along whatever lines social differentiation takes. Thus persons and groups within a society may view themselves and each other differently and even competitively, and subculture may become counterculture. Here, too, enters the element of power—the power of a person or group to impose his or its culture of inequality upon others.

From this broadly Weberian perspective, perhaps the fundamental questions concern the future of the political system. If a new dominant social consciousness develops, which involves the specification of political conflict groups organized on a basis of class or race, this is a development which is likely to begin within the established political structure. It is politicians who have the means to redefine their constituencies, and to alter the rules of the political game. In all developing countries the critical structural weaknesses show up most clearly within the political system; and in any modern state it is those who control the political institutions who have the greatest impact upon social change.

I begin by considering what might be called the radical critique of Jamaican society. It is associated with some social scientists in the University of the West Indies, and its view is that the two-party system is only shakily established in Jamaica, and liable to collapse. The argument, in essence, is that the system has been manipulated for the benefit of the capitalists and their middle-class allies; that consequently the working-class and the mass of the poor have become increasingly alienated; and that a violent confrontation is building up which will result in the overthrow of the present system.

The view depends upon the belief that the mass of Jamaicans have a common, objective interest in the overthrow of the present system, which is a complicated trick to deprive them of their fair share of Jamaica's economic wealth. They will be brought to a recognition of this objective interest through the development of a third party/union, and this understanding will be crystallized through the inevitably violent reaction of the 'power structure' to any serious challenge. The movement will be accompanied by a militant assertion of an 'African' cultural identity, for this is necessary to the realization that Jamaican society is presently constituted for the perpetuation of alien domination, false values, and the exclusion of the poor, predominantly black masses. [2]

The attention of these writers is directed particularly towards the Rastafarians, who seem to embody this new consciousness, and who have rejected 'the system', or, as the Rastafarians would put it, 'Babylon'. This is dangerous for a Marxist, of course, since in classical theory the lumpenproletariat cannot provide a base for effective working-class mobilization. [3] In fact they often fall into the trap of simply taking the old establishment bogeyman and making him a hope for change. I have already suggested that the Rastafarians, or some substitute figure of dangerous, almost lunatic, violence will always serve Jamaicans in their self-definition. This does not mean that Rastafarians, organized criminals, etc. are serious forces for social and political change.

The more general argument of these writers, that the mass of the people is becoming alienated from the political system, is difficult to sustain in view of the high level of commitment to the parties, and voting. On the contrary, voting figures over the years strongly suggest that the system has become strongly entrenched, and legitimate. Further, the steadiness of the 'swings' at elections seem, in comparative terms, to be a good indication of stability. As Professor Lipset pointed out, [4] the more cohesive and stable a democratic system is, the more likely it becomes that all segments of the population will react in the same direction to major stimuli; that is, if conditions facilitate the growth of leftist opinion, the socialists will gain votes among both the well-to-do and the workers, although they will remain relatively weaker in the upper strata. In the same way, during a period of right-wing ascendancy conservative votes will increase among the poorer groups.

Nor has there been the increase in repression which Dr Munroe, for example, confidently predicted.[5] I do not think that the 'war on gunmen' can be interpreted in these terms and, as Dr Stone found,[6]

> the nature of crime in the poor urban communities is such that police vigilance enjoys some community support. In spite of the excessive violence and arrogant use of power exercised by the police, the level of hostility to the police force is far lower than would be expected. ... It is therefore evident that criminality significantly erodes the potential political influence of the 'lumpen'.

The possibility of general mobilization on a basis of 'black' or 'African' consciousness is also a common theme of these writers, and others dealing with Jamaica, but once again it appears, to me, to depend upon a fundamental misunderstanding. At times they simply deceive themselves. Thus Dr Munroe, writing of the challenge of the Black Power PPP in 1962 correctly stressed the exaggerated fears which the party caused among elements of the middle-class establishment. However, he did not attempt to account for the fact that all sixteen PPP candidates lost their deposits at the election. Their meetings were spectacular and emotional, but their electoral support nugatory. This would seem to undermine the basic hypothesis, since the PPP attempted precisely to generate a black racial/working-class appeal.[7]

Nevertheless, there is an issue here which deserves reconsideration. It is difficult to define, but is perhaps best called the revolution in the expression of attitudes to status—via the various Rastafarian movements, Black Power politics, aggression towards the rich and the racial and ethnic minorities, etc. The difficulty of defining this issue is due to the fact that as it emerges in intellectual debate, it is essentially a 'middle-class' reflection upon a process occurring among the poor: and so it is distorted. To simplify, the past three decades have seen a revolution in attitudes towards the legitimacy of claims based upon 'race' or 'English' cultural attributes. Political communication between the poor and the élite leader has often been in terms of an idiom of 'African' assertion. Religious expression among the urban poor has been greatly influenced by Rastafarian ideas. Social expression is today, particularly among young men in town, often deliberately aggressive towards outsiders. In short, the symbolic statements many people make about the social structure have a new, aggressive form, and imply the assertion of 'African' racial/cultural identity. The distortion in middle-class perception derives from a failure to realize the situational meanings of such assertions; the record of the polls should indicate clearly enough that they do not imply a rejection of Jamaica's political leaders, or what they stand for. These modes of communication have entered the political arena mainly as a means of claiming support, a basis for identification. The minorities may be right to fear the potential of these tendencies being realized in racial scapegoating, but they cannot result in a mass movement against the political establishment, or Jamaican entrepreneurs, much less the established 'middle-class', because the self-definition involved in these symbolic assertions does not predicate the existence of a racially discriminatory political system. The racial model of Jamaica, never dominant since the Second World War at least, has been undermined by the operation of the two-party system and the overall transformation of the political structure since 1944. The 'anti-Jamaica' of the Rastafarians is a poor guide to the Jamaica of the future.

There are other possibilities of political revolution which need to be considered, most obviously a coup of some kind, supported by the army and police. This might occur in the context of widespread popular rioting; or it might occur in reaction to radical governmental measures, perhaps with foreign support; or it may be initiated by the governing party or the opposition in an attempt to impose one-party rule. The two main safeguards against such a development are the multi-class, national support enjoyed by the two parties, which preclude ready mobilization for such an attempt; and the existence of a strong professional class, particularly the legal profession, and also strong business interests, outside the political system and divided between the two parties.

In my view the present political system can be expected to persist. The main arguments in favour of this view have already been presented, and may be summed up briefly:

(i) The mass of the population is identified with the parties.

(ii) They are strongly influenced by middle-class leaders, including professional politicians, but also including a large number of men who act as effective intermediaries without being bound to the perpetual service of a party.

(iii) Organized labour is integrated with the two parties, and helps provide a stable balance while at the same time satisfying basic material aspirations.

(iv) Because the system has worked for thirty years, there is a strong expectation that it will continue to work. Thus supporters of the opposition party have a realistic hope that their party will be returned to power, and that then things will improve.

(v) A consequence of 'middle-class' influence and independence, and of the alternation of the parties in office, is the persistence of strong institutions outside the political arena, which also serve to hold the ring within which political competition takes place. One such is the judiciary, supported by a wealthy and independent legal profession, and a police force reasonably free of political bias and corruption. Another is the commercial community, with its strong foreign links, and a powerful voice in the national press. To put it another way, the very success of the two-party system has limited governmental power, and this in turn has allowed the persistence of institutions which inhibit extreme political competition. This is because the limitation of governmental power has permitted the persistence of areas of activity outside politics with rich material and status rewards.

There are, of course, also a number of important ideological supports. Some have been outlined already; I shall cite one more. It is based upon the accident that Bustamante, the Manleys, and Shearer are all considered by the Jamaican voter to be 'family'. Consequently people feel that no party leader will tolerate the forcible suppression of his rival, and that despite open conflict the opposing leaders will occasionally turn to one another for advice. A current myth will illustrate these beliefs. In 1967, Michael Manley narrowly held his parliamentary seat. It is widely belived that in fact he lost, but his old cousin, Bustamante, insisted that his favourite young relative should remain in parliament, and prevailed upon the JLP to permit this. In 1972, Shearer only narrowly held *his* seat. Again it is widely believed that he really lost it, but Bustamante persuaded Michael Manley, as a quid pro quo, to ensure that his 'son' should remain in Parliament.

Such notions clearly reflect a general belief in the limitation of political competition as a consequence of shared values and interests. Moreover, except among a few radical intellectuals, Jamaicans generally approve of this aspect of their political system. (On a broader level, the radicals argue that the similarity in party platforms reflects the failure of the parties to embody popular aspirations, and so enhance 'alienation'. It would be more reasonable to see this convergence as the inevitable product of a stable democratic system.) Emotions run high at election time, and violence is commonplace. Jamaica is a violent country. None the less, even at these times there are limits. Electoral fraud with the support of strong-arm men is rare, and appeal to the courts quick. Only one candidate has ever been killed.

The late Norman Manley summed up the basic conditions for the stability of the system, as he saw them, in his final political speech, his farewell address to a PNP rally in 1969:[8]

> There is, as of now, no dictatorship in Jamaica. There (are), as of now, two strong parties who believe in themselves and whose members believe in them. Between us we control the majority of the people in Jamaica. There is no great political vacuum in this country. The majority of the people are either members of the People's National Party or members of the Jamaica Labour Party. When you add to that fact that we have a loyal police force and a loyal army and that our courts are working in a fair and honest way, you will find that not one of the classic conditions, that make revolution possible, are present in Jamaica today.
>
> I remind you of one more thing. Where are we in the world? In the Caribbean area. You have seen America when Russia chose to go into Czechoslovakia and put down

liberalism—the American Government never said a
mumbling word. The Russians put 200,000 soldiers there.
When the revolution comes to Jamaica and the Prime
Minister of Jamaica says to the President of America, send
up an army to save us in this part of the world, do you
think he would refuse?

Well, perhaps he would; perhaps he would accept a coup against
certain kinds of government in Jamaica. But as my analysis
suggests, Manley did not go far enough in specifying the conditions
favouring the stability of the political system.

To a certain extent, my own argument may appear circular—
the establishment of the two-party system generated a series of
supports which permit its perpetuation. It is not a circular
argument, however, for my basic assumption is that the successful
establishment *and* perpetuation of the two-party system depended,
and depend today, upon features of Jamaica's social structure.
The key features in this context are the absence of solidary racial,
ethnic or class blocs of significance; and the presence of firmly-
grounded institutions of control outside the immediate political
arena. I consider the first point of greatest importance, and I
regard the very nature of the political system as the best possible
validation of my analysis of the social structure; and also as the
crucial condition for its persistence in its present form.

Analyses of Jamaican society which begin by assuming that the
society is divided into blocs, whether classes or the strata of
plural society theory, stumble, inevitably, when they try to
account for the modern development of the political system.
They are forced to depict it as a Machiavellian fraud, which
cannot persist. In my analysis it is a logical, though not inevitable
product of social conditions and social consciousness; and the
longer it persists the stronger my analysis must appear.

This does not mean that governments will not introduce reforms
and changes which could have important repercussions. Changes
are indeed very likely, particularly with respect to the distribution
of land and the general reform of the agricultural sector. My thesis
is rather that changes will be contained within the present institutional arrangements.

Notes

Chapter 1   Introduction

1 See particularly M. G. Smith, *The Plural Society in the British West Indies*; Edith Clarke, *My Mother Who Fathered Me*; and Fernando Henriques, *Family and Colour in Jamaica*. An excellent account also from the immediate post-war period, is provided by the English social psychologist Madeline Kerr, *Personality and Conflict in Jamaica*.

2 The major studies are Edward Brathwaite, *The Development of Creole Society in Jamaica: 1770–1820*; Philip Curtin, *Two Jamaicas: the role of ideas in a tropical colony 1830–1865*; Douglas Hall, *Free Jamaica 1838–1865—an economic history*; and Orlando Patterson, *The Sociology of Slavery*.

3 See Douglas Hall, *Free Jamaica*; Gisela Eisner, *Jamaica 1830–1930; a study in economic growth*; and David Lowenthal, 'Free coloured West Indians: a racial dilemma'.

Chapter 2   The Population of Jamaica

1 O. C. Francis, *The People of Modern Jamaica*, pp. 2–18.

2 In fact, the demographers have consistently underestimated emigration, and so their population projections have tended to be too high. See e.g. G. W. Roberts and D. O. Mills, 'Study of external migration affecting Jamaica: 1953–55', p. 112.

3 See L. Alan Eyre, *Geographic Aspects of Population Dynamics in Jamaica*, p. 23.

4 Stuart B. Philpott, *West Indian Migration: the Montserrat case*.

5 Gene Tidrick, 'Some aspects of Jamiacan emigration to the United Kingdom 1953–62', p. 39.

6 See Roberts and Mills, op. cit.; R. B. Davison, *West Indian migrants: social and economic facts of migration from the West Indies;* and O. C. Francis, 'The characteristics of emigrants just prior to changes in British Commonwealth immigration policy'.

7 In 1972, 7,000 Jamaican women emigrated to the USA as against 6,400 men. The disproportion is therefore not great.

8 Sources: *Economic Survey*, 1972; *Second Five Year Plan, 1970–75.*

9 J. R. Buffenmeyer, 'Emigration of high-level manpower and national development: a case-study of Jamaica', p. 137.

10 Ibid., p. 148.

Chapter 3   The Economy

1 In 1972, primary products accounted for 31 per cent of all exports, semi-processed products for 53 per cent, and manufactured goods for 16 per cent. Within the primary products category, bauxite accounted for 77 per cent, and export agriculture for 22 per cent. Within the semi-processed products category, alumina accounted for 77 per cent, and unrefined sugar and molasses for 22 per cent. Thus over three-quarters of primary and semi-processed exports are provided by the bauxite industry, and less than one-quarter by agriculture.

2 *Economic Survey*, Jamaica, 1972.

3 Owen Jefferson, *The Post-war Economic Development of Jamaica*, pp. 42 ff.

4 *Our Tourist Industry*, Facts on Jamaica, prepared by the Jamaica Tourist Board and the Jamaica Information Service.

5 *National Plan, 1970–75*. The 1968 figures are estimates.

6 The earlier estimate was provided by E. Ahiram, 'Income Distribution in Jamaica and Trinidad–Tobago' p. 7; the later is in Owen Jefferson, 'Is the Jamaican economy developing?', p. 6.

7 Ibid., p. 4.

Chapter 4   Agriculture

1 See M. Craton and J. Walvin, *A Jamaican Plantation: the history of Worthy Park, 1670–1970*; Hugh Paget, 'The free village system in Jamaica'; and for the long-established role of the small trader in agricultural products, see Margaret Katzin, 'The business of higglering in Jamaica'.

2 Statistics are derived mainly from the *Census of Agriculture, 1968–69*, chapter 4 of Owen Jefferson's *The Post-war Economic Development of Jamaica*, and the *Agricultural Sector Study, 1973*. Other source of statistics are mentioned below.

3 In 1963 René Dumont issued a dramatic warning (*Report to the Government of Jamaica on Planning Agricultural Development*, p. 33): The extensive ranch, grazed by free-roaming cattle, requires practically no labour input. It creates unemployment, or drives

manpower off the plains and on to the little-accessible slopes. This system of production, rational in the Rocky Mountains of the U.S.A., with a population density of less than one per square mile, becomes absolutely unacceptable in Jamaica. It should be remembered that the marked underutilization of manpower and land by the extensive ranch, which generates unemployment and excessive food imports, was one of the chief causes of the Cuban revolution.

4 If all this land was allocated to farmers with under 25 acres, it would account for no less than 22 per cent of the acreage in such farms today. See I. Johnson *et al.*, *A Review of Land Settlement in Jamaica*.

5 There is an excellent account of small-farming, still valid though the data is twenty years old—David Edwards, *Report on an Economic Study of Small Farming in Jamaica*.

Chapter 5   Employment and Migration to the Towns

1 Gene Tidrick, *Wages, Output and the Employment Lag in Jamaica*.
2 Marshall Hall, 'An analysis of the determinants of money wage changes in Jamaica 1958–64'.
3 Nassau Adams, 'Internal migration in Jamaica: an economic analysis'.
4 O. C. Francis, *The People of Modern Jamaica*, pp. 8–15.
5 Ibid., pp. 7–59. These figures are for employment in all these industries throughout the island by parish-born vs. non-parish-born. However, employment in these industries is concentrated strongly in the towns, particularly Kingston, Montego Bay, Spanish Town and May Pen.
6 The conclusion is drawn from two surveys carried out by the Department of Statistics, in 1967 and 1969—the first in Trench Town, the second in Delacree Pen.
7 Francis, op. cit., pp. 8–11.
8 See the surveys of the Department of Statistics of housing conditions in Trench Town and Delacree Pen.
9 Francis, op. cit., pp. 9–13.
10 *Agricultural Sector Study, 1973*.
11 *Survey of Agricultural Production on Holdings farmed by Alcan tenants*.
12 See Edith Clarke, *My Mother Who Fathered Me*, chapter 2.
13 Francis, op. cit., pp. 7–27.

Chapter 6   Economic Development and Social Change

1 Owen Jefferson, *The Post-war Economic Development of Jamaica*, p. 52.
2 E. Ahiram, 'Income distribution in Jamaica and Trinidad–Tobago', p. 6.
3 Ibid., p. 4. International comparisons of this kind are, however, notoriously misleading.
4 See G. E. Cumper, 'Incomes of upper 2·5 per cent and 8·5 per cent of income tax payers in relation to national income, Jamaica, 1951–65'; and Wolf Scott, *Report on a Study of the Levels of Living in Jamaica*.
5 Ahiram, op. cit., pp. 9–10.
6 Scott, op. cit., p. 13.
7 Shortly after coming to power in 1972, the PNP government instituted a commission of enquiry into allegations of corruption in the previous JLP administration. The findings were trivial, and while some scandals may have been too hot to handle, the situation was obviously by no means out of hand. The present administration has so far been remarkably free from scandal.

Chapter 7   Social Structure and Social Change

1 See Leo Kuper, *An African Bourgeoisie*. A number of these issues are, of course, central to the 'plural society' debate, which will be referred to once again in another chapter. The basic source of modern plural society theory is *Pluralism in Africa*, edited by Leo Kuper and M. G. Smith.

Chapter 8   Orthodox Models and the Traditional System—the Nineteenth Century

1 M. G. Smith, *The Plural Society in the British West Indies*, chapter 5. Quotations from pp. 111–12.
2 M. G. Smith, *Corporations and Society*, chapter 9.
3 Leonard Broom, 'The social differentiation of Jamaica', p. 117, where a lot of other useful evidence is briefly cited.
4 Quoted by David Lowenthal, in his very relevant essay, 'Free coloured West Indians'.
5 Clinton Black, *History of Jamaica*, p. 183.
6 Philip Curtin, *Two Jamaicas: the role of ideas in a tropical colony 1830–1865*, pp. 45–6.
7 Quoted by Curtin, op. cit., p. 202.
8 Quoted by Broom, op. cit., p. 119.

9 Edward Brathwaite, *The Development of Creole Society in Jamaica, 1770–1820*, chapter 15. He cites Smith in justification of his enterprise.
10 Curtin, op. cit., pp. 172–3.

Chapter 9 The Last Generation

1 M. G. Smith, *The Plural Society in the British West Indies*, chapter 7, quotations from pp. 163–4.
2 Op. cit., p. 175.
3 Loc. cit.
4 Fernando Henriques, *Family and Colour in Jamaica*, p. 42.
5 Op. cit., p. 46.
6 Op. cit., p. 53.
7 Op. cit., p. 63.
8 Madeline Kerr, *Personality and Conflict in Jamaica*, p. x.
9 Philip Curtin, *Two Jamaicas*, see, e.g., pp. 172–3.
10 Henriques, op. cit., p. 47.
11 Quoted by F. G. Cassidy, *Jamaica Talk*, p. 155.
12 Kerr, op. cit., pp. 96–7.
13 Elsa Goveia, *A Study on the Historiography of the British West Indies to the end of the Nineteenth Century*.
14 *Daily Gleaner*, 1966, quoted by Leonard Barrett, *The Rastafarians: a study in messianic cultism in Jamaica*, p. 164.
15 'A call for something to be done for the middle-class consumer has been made by the National Consumers League, in response to the Prime Minister's "Independence Package" of economic aid to the low-income groups. Mrs. Vie Mendes, president of the League, in a statement on behalf of her organization, noted that the middle-class consumers were made up of lower socio-economic groups.' *Jamaican Weekly Gleaner*, 14 August, 1974.
16 Councill Taylor, *Colour and Class: a comparative study of Jamaican status groups*, quotations from pp. 343–4.
17 Robert Ellis, 'Social stratification and social relations: an empirical test of the disjunctiveness of social classes', p. 574.

Chapter 10 Race and Class—Objective Indices

1 David Lowenthal, *West Indian Societies*, p. 94.
2 O. C. Francis, *The Population of Jamaica*, 4–2.
3 Loc. cit.
4 Leonard Broom, 'The social differentiation of Jamaica'.
5 Carl Stone, *Class, Race and Political Behaviour in Urban Jamaica*, quotation from p. 11.

Chapter 11   The Educational System

1 M. G. Smith, 'Towards a policy for Jamaican education—some notes', p. 7. According to census figures, 84 per cent of the population over the age of 10 could read and write in 1960. This was up from 74 per cent in 1943, and 58 per cent in 1921. However, the standards measured are very low.

2 *Economic Survey, 1972: Facts on Jamaica: Education.* 37·5 per cent also passed in applied mathematics, but only 8 candidates sat the examination.

3 K. Tidrick, 'Need for achievement, social class, and intention to emigrate in Jamaican students'.

4 D. R. Manley, 'Mental ability in Jamaica', p. 58. See also his paper, 'The school certificate examination, Jamaica, 1962'.

5 Manley, 'Mental ability in Jamaica', p. 65.

6 L. Alan Eyre, *Environment and education*, p. 29.

7 See M. G. Smith, *The Plural Society in the British West Indies,* chapter 9; Nancy Foner, *Status and Power in Rural Jamaica: a study of educational and political change*; and Kenneth V. M. Anderson, 'An analysis of certain factors affecting the scholastic achievement of lower socio-economic as compared with middle socio-economic children in Jamaica'.

8 See Edward Seaga, 'Parent–teacher relationships in a Jamaican village', and Nancy Foner, op. cit.

Chapter 12   A Village in the Hills

1 Other published community studies in Jamaica include Edith Clarke's *My Mother Who Fathered Me: a study of the family in three selected communities in Jamaica*; Yehudi Cohen's studies, reported in a series of papers; G. E. Cumper, 'A modern Jamaican sugar estate'; and Nancy Foner, *Status and Power in Rural Jamaica*.

2 A study of the area has been published by G. J. Kruijer, *Sociological Report on the Christiana Area*. There is also a paper on the Christiana upper-classes, Robert Ellis's 'Social status and social distance'. An excellent study of small-scale farmers, including a specific study of an area including D . . . , is a publication of the Agricultural Planning Unit, *Self-supporting Loan Scheme: survey of farms in the pilot areas*.

3 A rather formalistic account of peasant social stratification may be found in M. G. Smith and G. J. Kruijer, *A Sociological Manual for Extension Workers in the Caribbean*; it is repeated in Kruijer's study of Christiana cited above.

4 Madeline Kerr, *Personality and Conflict in Jamaica*, quotation from p. 96.

5 Schoolmasters are often lay preachers.

6 The figures are provided, broken down by polling stations, in the Reports of the Chief Electoral Officer. A similar situation in a north coast community is briefly sketched by Foner, in *Status and Power in Rural Jamaica*.

Chapter 13　Kingston and its Slums

1 Clarke's thesis was entitled 'Aspects of the urban geography of Kingston, Jamaica'. A monograph based on the thesis is in press, and some of the material is presented in a paper, 'An overcrowded metropolis: Kingston, Jamaica'.

2 Clarke (thesis), p. 331.

3 Ibid., pp. 357, 359.

4 Ibid., p. 377.

5 Clarke, 'An overcrowded metropolis: Kingston, Jamaica', p. 317.

6 M. H. Beaubrun, 'The pros and cons of cannabis use in Jamaica', and R. Prince, R. Greenfield and J. Marriott, 'Cannabis or alcohol? Observations on their use in Jamaica'.

7 The others are the founders of the two main parties, who led Jamaica into independence, and the two martyrs of the Morant Bay Rebellion, their black religious leader and the coloured parliamentarian who supported them.

8 See G. E. Simpson, 'Political cultism in West Kingston, Jamaica', and 'Jamaican revivalist cults'.

9 Leonard E. Barrett, *The Rastafarians: a study in messianic cultism in Jamaica*, p. 128. This study provides the fullest description of Rastafarian beliefs and practices, but focuses on an extreme branch of the movement.

10 M. G. Smith, Roy Augier and Rex Nettleford, 'The Ras Tafari Movement in Kingston, Jamaica'.

11 Rex Nettleford, *Mirror, Mirror: identity, race and protest in Jamaica*, pp. 39–113.

12 A survey published in 1965 suggested that while influential Jamaicans perceived the masses as threatening, poor Jamaicans did not reciprocate their feeling of social distance and fear or dislike; on the contrary, they provided, often, models of achievement. See J. Mau, 'The threatening masses: myth or reality?'

Chapter 14   Race and the Changing Jamaica—Public and Private Contexts

1 Olive Senior, *The Message is Change: a perspective on the 1972 general election,* p. 62.
2 Ibid., pp. 65–6.
3 Rex Nettleford, *Mirror, Mirror: identity, race and protest in Jamaica.*
4 Louise Bennett, *Jamaica Labrish,* p. 179. I am grateful to the author for permission to quote this passage.

Chapter 15   The Two-party System

1 Other new states have claims to be democratic. India and Israel have multi-party systems and proportional representation, but both have been governed by one party (usually in coalition) since independence. Tanzania and, with perhaps less justification, some other countries can claim to have a form of single-party democracy. In some other states there are elements of a two-party system, but changes in government have tended to require the application of force, as in Ceylon and Guyana.
2 A former JLP minister, Mr Lightbourne, was returned on the JLP ticket in 1972, but subsequently left his party and remained in parliament as an independent. He has started a party of his own, which had some successes in his constituency in the recent local government elections. However, this is still a very limited regional success, and considering Mr Lightbourne's advanced age, and the failure of his party to organize elsewhere, it is unlikely to break the two-party pattern.
3 Mike Morrissey, 'A spatial analysis of Jamaica's general elections in 1967 and 1972', pp. 19–22.
4 Ibid., pp. 9–13.
5 See Trevor Munroe, *The Politics of Constitutional Decolonization: Jamaica, 1944–62.* This is the fullest account of the emergence of the two-party system, but it is written from a position of strong political commitment which often biasses the argument.
6 M. Faber, 'A "swing" analysis of the Jamaican election of 1962: a note'.
7 This is purely hypothetical, since the constituencies have been redrawn, and the voters' rolls radically revised and enlarged, particularly as a result of extending the vote to eighteen-year-olds.
8 Morrissey, op. cit., p. 30; Faber, op. cit.
9 Nancy Foner briefly reports a similar situation in another rural area —*Status and Power in Rural Jamaica.*

10 Carl Stone, *Class, Race and Political Behaviour in Urban Jamaica*, chapter 4.
11 Stone, op. cit., p. 43.
12 For example, Jean Blondel cites the following figures, which indicate the relationship between 'class' and party preference in Britain, specifically for 1958, but, he argues, generally for the 1950s and 1960s:

	Conservative	Labour	Other
Solid middle-class	85	10	5
Lower middle-class	70	25	5
Upper working-class (manual)	35	60	5
Solid working-class	30	65	5

(Jean Blondel, *Voters, Parties and Leaders: the social fabric of British politics*, p. 55.)
13 Stone, op. cit., p. 46.

Chapter 16   Middle-class Leadership

1 Paul Robertson, 'Party "organization" in Jamaica'.
Summing up the situation in 'Coco Hill', Nancy Foner wrote (*Status and Power in Rural Jamaica*, p. 124. See chapter 7 in detail):
The local branches of the national parties are designed to consolidate rural support by building strong local organizations, that is, by recruiting new members and retaining old ones through the promises of concrete benefits, and making sure that these members vote on Election Day. The parties do not offer the villagers the opportunity to occupy prestigious and influential political roles in the society and their major function is the distribution of patronage to supporters.
2 M. G. Smith provides a superb definition and description of the community in rural Jamaica in his essay, 'Community Organization in Rural Jamaica', reprinted as chapter 8 of *The Plural Society in the British West Indies*.
3 C. Paul Bradley, 'Mass parties in Jamaica: structure and organization'. A useful source is O. W. Phelps, 'Rise of the Labour Movement in Jamaica'.

Chapter 17   Policy-making

1 Carl Stone, *Class, Race and Political Behaviour in Urban Jamaica*, pp. 149–51.

Chapter 18 Political Mobilization and Social Change

1 Lloyd A. Fallers, *Inequality: social stratification reconsidered*, chapter 1, quotation from pp. 5–6.

2 See Trevor Munroe, *The politics of constitutional decolonization: Jamaica 1944–62*; Paul Robertson, 'Party "organization" in Jamaica'; and Carl Stone, *Class, Race and Political Behaviour in Urban Jamaica*. A similar line of argument dominated the now defunct journal, *Abeng*, and the journal and other publications of the 'New World' group.

3 Stone, op. cit., pp. 146–55, provides an interesting discussion of the political beliefs and potential of the lumpenproletariat.

4 Seymour Martin Lipset, *Political Man*, p. 33.

5 Munroe, op. cit., pp. 210–19.

6 Stone, op. cit., p. 152.

7 Munroe, op. cit., p. 164.

8 Norman Washington Manley, *Manley and The New Jamaica: selected speeches and writings*, pp. 382 ff.

Bibliography

Abbreviations

SES   *Social and Economic Studies* (University of the West Indies).
ISER   Institute of Social and Economic Research (University of the West Indies).

Official (unsigned)

Agriculture Sector Study, 1973, Ministry of Agriculture.
Census of Agriculture, 1968–69, Ministry of Agriculture.
Economic Survey, National Planning Agency, annually.
Facts on Jamaica: Education, Dept of Statistics, 1968.
Facts on Jamaica: Our Tourist Industry, Dept of Statistics, and Tourist Board, 1972.
Labour Force Survey, Dept of Statistics, 1968.
The Labour Force, 1972, Dept of Statistics.
Second Five Year Plan, 1970–75, National Planning Agency.
Self-supporting Loan Scheme: survey of farms in the pilot areas, Ministry of Agriculture, 1969.
A Survey of Housing Conditions in Trench Town, Dept of Statistics, 1967.
A Survey of Housing Conditions in Delacree Pen, Dept of Statistics, 1969.
Survey of Agricultural Production on Holdings farmed by Alcan tenants, Alcan Jamaica Ltd, Jamaica, 1972.

Books, articles and signed reports

ADAMS, NASSAU A., 'Internal migration in Jamaica: an economic analysis', *SES*, vol. 18, no. 2, 1969, pp. 137–51.

AHIRAM, R., 'Income distribution in Jamaica and Trinidad–Tobago', in *The Caribbean in Transition*, ed. F. M. Andic, and T. G. Mathews, Institute of Caribbean Studies, University of Puerto Rico, 1965, pp. 1–11.

ANDERSON, KENNETH V. MCLEAN, 'An analysis of certain factors affecting the scholastic achievement of lower socio-economic as compared with middle socio-economic children in Jamaica', Ed.D. thesis, Cornell University, 1966 (unpublished).

156

BARRETT, LEONARD E., *The Rastafarians: a study in messianic cultism in Jamaica*, Institute of Caribbean Studies, University of Puerto Rico, 1968.

BEAUBRUN, M. H., 'The Pros and Cons of Cannabis Use in Jamaica', *Newsletter, Carib. Psychiat. Assoc.*, vol. 2, no. 2, pp. 3–8.

BENNETT, LOUISE, *Jamaica Labrish*, Sangster, Kingston, 1966.

BLACK, CLINTON V., *History of Jamaica* (3rd edition), Collins, London, 1965.

BLONDEL, JEAN, *Voters, Parties and Leaders: the social fabric of British politics*, Penguin, Harmondsworth, 1953.

BRADLEY, C. PAUL, 'Mass parties in Jamaica: structure and organization', *SES*, vol. 9, no. 4, 1960, pp. 375–416.

BRATHWAITE, EDWARD, *The Development of Creole Society in Jamaica: 1770–1820*, Clarendon Press, Oxford, 1971.

BROOM, L., 'The social differentiation of Jamaica', *American Sociological Review*, vol. 19, no. 2, 1954, pp. 115–25.

BUFFENMEYER, J. R., 'Emigration of high-level manpower and national development: a case-study of Jamaica', Ph.D. thesis, University of Pittsburgh, 1970 (unpublished).

CASSIDY, FREDERIC G., *Jamaica Talk*, Macmillan, London, 1971.

CHEN-YOUNG, PAUL L., *Report on Private Investment in the Caribbean*, Atlas Publishing Co., Kingston, 1973.

CLARKE, C. G., 'Aspects of the urban geography of Kingston, Jamaica', D.Phil. thesis, Oxford University, 1967 (unpublished).

—— 'Population pressure in Kingston, Jamaica: a study of unemployment and overcrowding', *Transactions of the Institute of British Geographers*, 1966.

—— 'An overcrowded metropolis: Kingston, Jamaica', in *Geography and a Crowding World*, ed. R. Mansell Prothero, L. Kosinski and W. Zelinsky, Oxford University Press, New York, 1970.

CLARKE, EDITH, *My Mother Who Fathered Me: a study of the family in three selected communities in Jamaica*, Allen & Unwin, London, 1957.

COHEN, YEHUDI A., 'Four categories of interpersonal relationships in the family and community in a Jamaican village', *Anthropological Quarterly*, vol. 3, no. 4, 1955, pp. 121–47.

CRATON, M. and WALVIN, J., *A Jamaican Plantation: the history of Worthy Park 1670–1970*, London, 1970.

CUMPER, G. E., 'A modern Jamaican sugar estate', *SES*, vol. 3, no. 2, 1954, pp. 119–60.

—— 'Incomes of upper 2·5 per cent and 8·5 per cent of income tax payers in relation to national income, Jamaica, 1951–65', *SES*, vol. 20, no. 4, 1971, pp. 362–8.

CURTIN, PHILIP D., *Two Jamaicas: the role of ideas in a tropical colony 1830–1865*, Harvard University Press, 1955.

DAVISON, R. B., *West Indian Migrants: social and economic facts of migration from the West Indies*, Institute of Race Relations, Oxford University Press, London, 1962.

DUMONT, RENÉ, *Report to the Government of Jamaica on Planning Agricultural Development*, FAO, 1963.

EDWARDS, DAVID, *Report on an Economic Study of Small Farming in Jamaica*, ISER, 1961.

EISNER, GISELE, *Jamaica 1830–1930: A study in economic growth*, Manchester University Press, 1961.

ELLIS, ROBERT A., 'Social status and social distance', *Sociology and Social Research*, vol. 40, no. 4, 1956, p. 240.

EYRE, L. ALAN, 'Environment and education: a study of social and environmental factors in the patterns of education and attainment in a Jamaican parish (Manchester)', M.A., University of the West Indies, 1966 (unpublished).

—— *Geographic Aspects of Population Dynamics in Jamaica*, Florida Atlantic University Press, 1972.

FABER, MICHAEL, 'A "swing" analysis of the Jamaican election of 1962: a note', *SES*, vol. 4, 1964, pp. 302–10.

FALLERS, LLOYD A., *Inequality: social stratification reconsidered*, University of Chicago Press, 1973.

FONER, NANCY, *Status and Power in Rural Jamaica: a study of educational and political change*, Teachers College Press, Columbia University, 1973.

FRANCIS, O. C., *The People of Modern Jamaica*, Dept of Statistics, Kingston, 1963.

GOVEIA, E., *A Study on the Historiography of the British West Indies to the End of the Nineteenth Century*, Pan American Institute of Geography and History, Mexico, 1956.

HALL, DOUGLAS G., *Free Jamaica 1838–1865: an economic history*, Yale University Press, 1959.

HALL, MARSHALL, 'An analysis of the determinants of money wage changes in Jamaica 1958–64', *SES*, vol. 17, no. 2, 1968, pp. 133–46.

HENRIQUES, FERNANDO M., *Family and Colour in Jamaica*, Eyre & Spottiswoode, London, 1953.

JEFFERSON, OWEN, 'Is the Jamaican Economy Developing?', *New World*, vol. 5, no. 4, 1972, pp. 4–11.

—— *The Post-war Economic Development of Jamaica*, ISER, 1972.

JOHNSON, I. *et al.*, *A Review of Land Settlement in Jamaica*, Min. of Agriculture, Kingston, 1972.

KATZIN, MARGARET FISHER, 'The business of higglering in Jamaica', *SES*, vol. 9, no. 3, 1960, pp. 297–331.

KERR, MADELINE, *Personality and Conflict in Jamaica*, Collins, London, 1952.

KRUIJER, G. J., *Sociological Report on the Christiana Area*, Agricultural Information Service, Min. of Agriculture, Kingston, 1969.

KUPER, LEO, *An African Bourgeoisie: race, class and politics in South Africa*, Yale University Press, 1965.

KUPER, LEO and M. G. SMITH eds, *Pluralism in Africa*, University of California Press, 1969.

LIPSET, SEYMOUR MARTIN, *Political Man*, Heinemann, London, 1960.

LOWENTHAL, DAVID, *West Indian Societies*, Oxford University Press, London, 1972.

—— 'Free coloured West Indians: a racial dilemma', in *Studies in Eighteenth-century Culture*, vol. 3, *Racism in the Eighteenth Century*, The Press of Case Western Reserve University, 1973.

MANLEY, D. R., 'Mental ability in Jamaica', *SES*, vol. 12, no. 1, 1963.

—— 'The school certificate examination, Jamaica 1962', *SES*, vol. 18, no. 1, 1969.

MANLEY, NORMAN WASHINGTON, *Manley and The New Jamaica: Selected speeches and writings*, ed. Rex Nettleford, Longman Caribbean, 1971.

MAU, J., 'The threatening masses: myth or reality?' in *The Caribbean in Transition*, Institute of Caribbean Studies, University of Puerto Rico, 1965.

MILLER, ERROL L., 'Body image, physical beauty, and colour among Jamaican adolescents', *SES*, vol. 18, 1969.

MORRISSEY, MIKE, 'A spatial analysis of the 1967 and 1972 general elections in Jamaica', cyclostyled, Kingston, 1972.

MUNROE, TREVOR, *The Politics of Constitutional Decolonization: Jamaica 1944–62*, ISER, 1972.

NETTLEFORD, REX, *Mirror, Mirror: identity, race and protest in Jamaica*, Collins Sangster, Kingston, 1970.

PAGET, HUGH, 'The free village system in Jamaica', *CQ*, vol. 1, no. 4, 1954, pp. 7–19.

PATTERSON, H. ORLANDO, *The Sociology of Slavery*, MacGibbon & Kee, London, 1967.

PHELPS. O. W., 'Rise of the Labour Movement in Jamaica', *SES*, vol. 9, no. 4, 1960, pp. 417–68.

PHILPOTT, STUART B., *West Indian Migration: the Montserrat Case*, Athlone Press, London, 1973.

PRINCE, R., GREENFIELD, R. and MARRIOTT, J. 'Cannabis or Alcohol?

Observations on their use in Jamaica', *Bulletin on Narcotics,* vol. XXIV, no. 1, 1972, pp. 1–9.

ROBERTS, G. W. and MILLS, D. O., 'Study of external migration affecting Jamaica: 1953–55', supplement to *SES,* vol. 7, no. 2, 1958.

ROBERTSON, PAUL, 'Party "organization" in Jamaica', *SES,* vol. 21, no. 1, 1972, pp. 30–43.

SCOTT, WOLF, *Report on a Study of the Levels of Living in Jamaica,* United Nations for Government of Jamaica, 1966.

SEAGA, EDWARD P. G., 'Parent-teacher relationships in a Jamaican village', *SES,* vol. 4, 1955, pp. 289–302.

SENIOR, OLIVE, *The Message is Change: a perspective on the 1972 general elections,* Kingston Publishers Ltd, Kingston, 1972.

SIMPSON, G. E., 'Political cultism in West Kingston, Jamaica', *SES,* vol. 3, no. 4, 1955.

—— 'Jamaican revivalist cults', *SES,* vol. 5, no. 4, 1956.

SMITH, M. G., *The Plural Society in the British West Indies,* University of California Press, 1965.

—— 'Towards a policy for Jamaican education—some notes', 1973 (unpublished, cyclostyled).

—— *Corporations and Society,* Duckworth, London, 1974.

SMITH, M. G., AUGIER, ROY and NETTLEFORD, REX, *The Ras Tafari Movement in Kingston, Jamaica,* ISER, 1960.

SMITH, M. G. and KRUIJER, G. J., *A Sociological Manual for Extension Workers in the Caribbean,* University of the West Indies Department of Extra-Mural Studies, 1957.

STONE, CARL, *Class, Race and Political Behaviour in Urban Jamaica,* ISER, 1973.

TAYLOR, COUNCILL, 'Color and Class: A comparative study of Jamaican status groups', Ph.D. thesis, Yale University, 1955 (unpublished).

TIDRICK, GENE, 'Some aspects of Jamaican emigration to the United Kingdom 1953–62', *SES,* vol. 15, no. 1, 1966, pp. 22–39.

—— *Wages, Output and the Employment Lag in Jamaica,* research memo. no. 40, Center for Development Economics, Williams College, Mass., 1970.

TIDRICK, K., 'Need for achievement, social class, and intention to emigrate in Jamaican students', *SES,* vol. 20, no. 1, 1971, pp. 52–60.

Index

161

Index